Computer Graphics for Craft, Design and Technology

Robert Cater

King Edward VI Handsworth School

Longman Group UK Limited,
Longman House, Burnt Mill, Harlow,
Essex CM20 2JE, England
and Associated Companies throughout the world.

© Longman Group Limited 1988
All rights reserved; no part of this publication
may be reproduced, stored in a retrieval system,
or transmitted in any form or by any means, electronic,
mechanical, photocopying, recording, or otherwise,
without the prior written permission of the Publishers
or a licence permitting restricted copying issued
by the Copyright Licensing Agency Ltd,
33–34 Alfred Place, London WC1E 7DP.

First published 1988

Set in 10/12 point Helvetica, Linotron 202.

Produced by Longman Group (FE) Ltd
Printed in Hong Kong

ISBN 0 582 33103 X

Acknowledgements

The publishers are grateful to the following for permission to reproduce photographs and other copyright material:
Austin Rover, p. 9 (top left and right); Boxford, pp. 61 and 62; Computervision, p. 10 (top left); Electronic Arts — London, p. 9 (bottom left and right); Ford Motor Company, p. 10 (top right); P A Design Ltd for Hagenuk GmbH, Germany, p. 10 (cordless telephone — two images); P A Design Ltd for SEATCO, Belgium, p. 10 (aircraft seating); Prime Computer (UK), p. 9 (centre: three images) and car images on cover; Robo Systems, p. 68; TechSoft (Clwyd), p. 64; and Vehicle Design, p. 64 (top).

Contents

Notes for the teacher	v
1 Computer graphics	**1**
1.1 Early computers	1
1.2 Modern computer graphics	1
1.3 The purpose of this book	2
2 Graphics with the BBC micro	**3**
2.1 Creating graphics	3
2.2 Producing simple lines and shapes	3
2.3 The use of PROCEDURES in drawing	17
2.4 User-defined graphics	19
3 Creative patterns	**22**
3.1 Geometric patterns	22
3.2 Polygon patterns	25
3.3 Lissajous patterns	29
3.4 Some applications for the pattern-generating programs	32
3.5 Recursion	33
3.6 Filography	34
4 Interactive computer-aided drafting	**37**
4.1 The computer as a drafting device	37
4.2 Rubber banding	47
4.3 Pick and drag	47
4.4 An electronic circuit-drafting program	50
4.5 Isometric drawing	55
5 Commercial systems for schools	**59**
5.1 The AMX mouse	59
5.2 British Thornton Compas	61
5.3 Easidraw, Easicad and Easicam	62
5.4 Grafpad 2	63
5.5 Vehicle Design (Heinemann)	64
5.6 Designer (Techsoft, Clwyd)	64
5.7 Linear Graphics	64
5.8 MICAD (Heinemann)	66
5.9 Pineapple Software	66
5.10 Robocom Bitstik	67
Further reading	69
Glossary	70

Notes for the teacher

This book is intended to help pupils pursuing courses in craft, design and technology to include some computer graphics and computer-aided design into their coursework. Computer-aided design is now so widely used commercially that to ignore it within school-based design work would be to deprive our pupils of the opportunity to understand and familiarise themselves with a graphic utility which now has a major influence on the real world of design.

The book is written so that pupils with little or no understanding of computers can use the programs. It is hoped, however, that many will gain an understanding of the programs so that they can experiment with the ideas presented and possibly develop programs of their own. Most of the programs are relatively simple and are kept short so that they can easily be entered into the computer. All programs could be saved on disk or tape for future use, but, although there is something to be said for the confidence pupils gain in entering and manipulating shorter programs themselves, this is not so with the longer programs, which are included here as a resource, and as such should be saved on tape or disk for use by pupils. There is little educational value to be gained from pupils spending an inordinate amount of time entering longer, more complex programs.

The earlier programs are explained thoroughly so that pupils can gain an understanding of the fundamentals of programming to produce graphics on the BBC microcomputer. This should help them understand much of the programming used throughout the book. While it is hoped that many pupils will wish to understand the principle of programming for interactive graphics, it is also important to emphasise that some pupils may gain satisfaction from using the programs without understanding how they work.

Colour has not been featured in the programs in order to keep the programming principles as simple as possible. Moreover, I feel that the programs will be of greater use if they do not rely on colour. Although colour monitors are quite common now, they are much more expensive than mono visual display units and, in addition to this, good quality colour-printing facilities are not commonly available in schools. It could serve as a useful exercise if interested pupils adapted programs to include colour where schools have the facilities to benefit from this.

The hardware

The programs will work on the BBC B, B+ and Master 128 microcomputers. Graphic work with the computer is quite meaningless without the facility to obtain printed copies of drawings. If no equipment is available for producing paper copies of drawings images can be traced from the VDU on to layout or tracing paper using a soft grade pencil. This is quite a crude method, however, and most schools will probably have access to a dot matrix printer. These printers will reproduce screen graphic images in a characteristically bold form lacking line quality. They are, however, a good starting point and have the advantage that, with the use of a suitable ROM, they can be made to reproduce most screen images. The Computer Concepts Printmaster ROM has been suggested, but there are other commercial ROMs available which will offer this facility. The Printmaster ROM has many facilities but it is the *GDUMP command which is utilised here. If the ROM is fitted to one of the ROM sockets in the computer, this command can be used within programs to obtain a printout of all or part of the screen on an Epson or Epson-compatible printer.

The best way of obtaining good quality drawings from a computer is by using a plotter. This will draw lines with a pen using vectors produced from data provided by the computer. Some of the programs

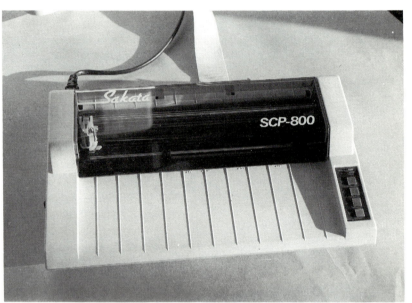

A Sakata plotter (MCP 40 type)

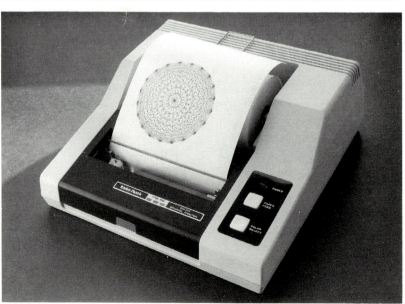

The Tandy TRS 80 plotter

are modified to suit the MCP 40, an inexpensive type of plotter which is sold under several brand names. Tandy shops sell a version which retails at a very reasonable price. The plotter is called the TRS 80, and it represents excellent value for money for introducing certain aspects of computer graphics. Most of the programs in Chapter 3 have a version which will produce a plotted image on the Tandy TRS 80. Many of the other ideas in the book can also be modified for this plotter. The plotter can be connected using a standard Epson-type parallel printer cable. The small DIP switch at the rear of the TRS 80 should be set so that switches 1 and 2 are in the off position and switches 3 and 4 are in the on position.

Some of the programs are also written so that they will plot images on a Plotmate plotter. This is more expensive, but it is a more sophisticated piece of equipment and, as such, offers better quality images on a larger paper size. This plotter is also much easier to program for the BBC computer as it uses the standard BBC BASIC graphics commands. The programs given are written to dump to a standard Plotmate using direct drive from the BBC printer part.

1 Computer graphics

1.1 Early computers

The computer, as a commercial product, has only been available for about 30 years. The early computers were so large that we would probably not recognise them as computers. To look at the compact high-tech computers we are familiar with today and compare them with the room full of valves, switches and wires needed to perform lesser operations in the 1950s makes us realise how quickly computer technology has evolved.

Computer graphics as we know them today are even younger. Very simple graphics were first produced in the 1960s and it has needed the development of the larger memories and faster processing power of more recent computers to get the more sophisticated graphics we are now growing used to. The use of Computer Aided Design (CAD) has developed rapidly in recent years due to the development of speed and quality in computer graphics generally.

The production and manipulation of graphic images is one of the most demanding applications for computers and requires vast amounts of memory space and fast processing power if anything but the most elementary **wire-frame** images are to be produced. The illustrations on pages 9 and 10 show some of the sophisticated computer images which are now being produced in various areas of the commercial design world.

1.2 Modern computer graphics

Computer graphics are now widely used, and it is not difficult to see examples. Many television captions and advertisements feature computer-generated graphics, and everyone will now be familiar with the computer graphics used in arcade games. The film industry also makes use of computers for special effects, and the Walt Disney film *Tron* is probably one of the best known examples.

The increase in processing power, which took place in the early 1980s, has enabled computer images to be truly three-dimensional with realistic colour and real-time movement. The most dramatic illustration of this is in the graphics produced in flight simulators to train aircraft pilots. The pilot can now sit in a simulator and have a computer-generated image of the view from an aircraft, which changes in response to his actions on the 'aircraft' controls. The ability to do this kind of thing will increase the use of computers in designing. Their capability now extends beyond the more analytical field of engineering wire-frame graphics to that of the stylists in the design studios. Designers can now use computers to produce their colour-rendered developmental drawings so that computer design systems will be used in all areas of designing. Product, fashion and textile designers already make effective use of this new technology to help save time and increase design flexibility.

Computer graphics offer many advantages to commercial users. If the system is suitable it will make the designers' work easier at the drawing stage, but after that there are many advantages offered by the electronic wizardry of the computer. Images can be modified, rotated, or set against different backgrounds at the touch of a button. Colours and patterns can be changed and lettering added with easy modification of type faces. These facilities, along with many others, can be accomplished quickly and easily with a computer system.

One exciting development has taken place in the car industry, where CAD systems are being linked to robot sculptors to produce life-sized models of cars from graphic images produced with a computer. The photographs on page 9 show this system in operation in the development of the Rover 800 at the Austin Rover plant in Longbridge.

The computer revolution has also increased the potential advantages offered by electronic information storage and transference. Large, complex drawings can now be kept in compact electronic storage systems for later retrieval. Any drawing can be loaded back into the computer and modified before being reproduced on a **plotter**, thus saving the time and money which would be required to reproduce similar drawings manually.

Drawings stored as **digital data** in computers can easily be transmitted to similar computers nationally or internationally using telephone lines. This has obvious advantages in the commercial world of design, and I expect many schools could benefit from this type of communication system if they could afford the necessary hardware. Imagine how convenient it would be if you could get drawings from libraries and other school pupils printed in your school, whenever you wanted them to help with research for a major design project.

1.3 The purpose of this book

This book will help you to understand how computer graphics are produced and will introduce some of the fundamental principles involved in many interactive CAD programs. You will not be able to produce complex drawings like those used in industry because the computers used in schools are not powerful enough.

The book is written for use with the BBC microcomputer, because so many schools have these machines. BBC computers are very versatile and are well suited to the work carried out in CDT departments, but they lack memory space and processing speed for all but the most elementary of three-dimensional graphics. There is, however, plenty of scope to develop an understanding of computer graphics and to use the computer as an additional design resource during your coursework.

2 Graphics with the BBC micro

2.1 Creating graphics

Computer graphics are produced by lighting up small rectangular areas on a screen, and the images produced depend on how the computer is programmed to light these small rectangles. The screen can be an ordinary domestic television or a computer monitor, but when used with a computer the display unit is often called a **visual display unit** (VDU for short). Each of the small, illuminated rectangular areas is called a **pixel**, and the number of pixels that the screen is divided into determines the clarity, or resolution, of the image the computer makes. The resolution indicates how many pixels are available on the screen and hence, how clear the screen image will be: high resolution means more pixels and a finer image, whereas low resolution means fewer pixels, resulting in a less well-defined image. Figure 2.1 shows how computer images are built up from the rectangular pixels. The BBC microcomputer uses a **graphics co-ordinate system** of 1280 × 1024, although the maximum pixel definition available is only half of this horizontally and a quarter vertically, giving maximum definition of 640 × 256.

Pixels are located on the screen using pairs of co-ordinates, where the first co-ordinate gives the distance across the screen and the second co-ordinate gives the distance up the screen. This system is called **the rectangular Cartesian set** and is frequently used for drawing graphs. It is similar to the system of locating a position on a map using grid references.

With the BBC micro and most others, the graphics origin is at the bottom left-hand corner of the screen. From this point two imaginary **axes** originate. The imaginary X axis runs horizontally across the bottom of the screen from left to right, and a Y axis up the left-hand edge of the screen. The X axis is 1280 units long and the Y axis 1024 units (Figure 2.2). A point in the centre of the screen would be 1280 ÷ 2 along the X axis and 1024 ÷ 2 up the Y axis. Thus the co-ordinates for a point in the centre of the screen will be 640,512 (Figure 2.3). Note that the X, or horizontal value of a point, is always given first, followed by a comma and then the Y value.

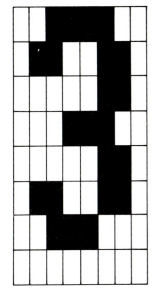

Figure 2.1

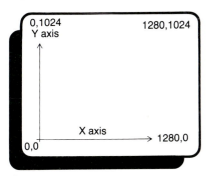

Figure 2.2

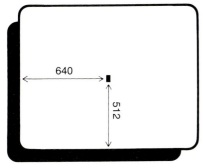

Figure 2.3

2.2 Producing simple lines and shapes

Before we try drawing on a computer we will need to understand a little more about how the BBC micro handles graphics. The BBC has eight MODES of operation numbered 0 to 7, and when switched on it is always in MODE 7. MODES 3,6 and 7 are text-only MODES, and graphics are produced in MODES 0,1,2,4 and 5. These MODES vary in resolution due to the different number of pixels offered by each.

The best-quality lines are obtained in MODE 0, which has a resolution of 640 × 256 pixels. MODE 1 offers medium resolution with 320 × 256 pixels. Each pixel is made up from a number of screen units. For example, in MODE 0, each pixel is made from a **matrix** of 2 × 4 screen co-ordinates. There are considerations other than the quality of the resolution, such as the memory and colours available, but these are not going to affect most of the graphics we will do in this book.

The important thing to remember is that the computer must be put into a MODE which supports graphics before any of the work in this book can be done. We will use MODE 0 quite a lot as it offers the highest resolution available on the BBC micro.

Now we can try lighting up a point in the middle of the screen. Before you begin there are some important things to remember:

- All commands are entered in capital letters.
- Do not confuse the numeral 0 with the capital letter O.
- Every command line must be followed by pressing the RETURN key which will be indicated as [RETURN]. First type

```
MODE 0 [RETURN]
```

The computer is now in a high resolution graphics mode. Now type:

```
PLOT 69,640,512 [RETURN]
```

This will illuminate a pixel in the centre of the screen. On the BBC machine PLOT 69 is the command to light one pixel at the point given by the co-ordinates following the command. Try lighting points in a variety of positions on the screen.

Line drawing

The PLOT 69 command would make it rather difficult to draw lines, so the BBC has the commands MOVE and DRAW to make it easier. When drawing with a pencil we need to be able to move around the graphics area without making a mark. The command MOVE X,Y moves the **cursor** (an imaginary pencil) to a point (X,Y) without creating an image on the screen. The command DRAW X,Y allows lines to be drawn from the current position of the cursor to the co-ordinates given by X,Y.

We can now try out these commands. If you still have pixels illuminated, clear the screen by typing the command:

```
CLS [RETURN]
```

This command clears the screen and can be used to give a blank screen to start a new drawing.

To draw a line from the centre of the screen to a point midway along the bottom of the screen we enter the following commands but **remember to press the [RETURN] key after each command**:

```
MODE 0
MOVE 640,512
DRAW 640,0
```

A vertical line will now appear from the centre of the screen to the

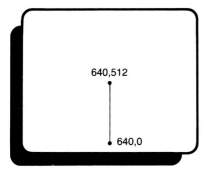

Figure 2.4

middle of the bottom edge. The MOVE command tells the computer to move the cursor, without leaving a screen image, to the point specified by the given co-ordinates, and the DRAW command tells the computer to draw a line from the point (640,512) to the new co-ordinates given after the DRAW statement (640,0) (Figure 2.4). You will notice that the point (640,0) is not right at the bottom of the screen. This is because the graphics window created by the computer does not use the full screen area.

Building programs

So far the computer has acted on each of our commands immediately the [RETURN] key is pressed. This does not use the memory capacity of the computer which allows us to program it to do things and store that program in its memory to be repeated if necessary. Let us convert the simple vertical line drawing exercise into a program.

To prepare a program we put a number before each command line and it is usual to step these numbers in increments of ten. This will allow you to insert other line numbers, if needed, when structuring more difficult programs. The program to draw the vertical line would be:

```
10 MODE 0
20 MOVE 640,512
30 DRAW 640,0
```

Now type

```
RUN [RETURN]
```

The screen will be cleared automatically when the computer operates the MODE 0 command in line 10, and then the vertical line will be drawn. The program listing has disappeared but it is still in the computer's memory and can be brought back on to the screen by typing LIST[RETURN] or L.[RETURN] which will also be accepted by the computer.

Now type CLS[RETURN] and NEW[RETURN]. The NEW command tells the computer to forget about the program that it has in its memory so that we can enter a new program without worrying about information from a previous program affecting the new one.

Here is a program to draw a square in the bottom left corner of the screen.

```
10 MODE 0
20 DRAW 200,0
30 DRAW 200,200
40 DRAW 0,200
50 DRAW 0,0
```

RUN the program. Note that no MOVE command is needed at the beginning of the program because the cursor starts at the origin (0,0) which is the start of the square in this case. If the square is to appear in another position then a MOVE statement would be needed as the first instruction line.

Exercises
1 Write a program to draw a square of 300 units in the centre of the screen. If you produce a grid sheet like the one given below (Figure 2.5) it will help you work out the co-ordinates.
2 Write a program to draw a square at each corner of the screen.

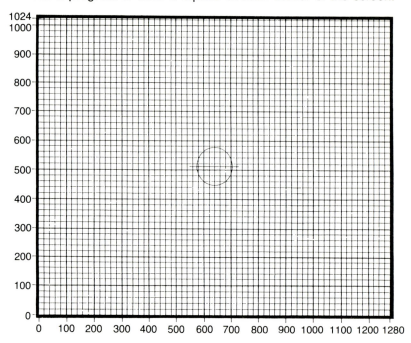

Figure 2.5

Producing printing on the screen

The computer will print things on the screen as you type them on the keyboard, but to produce information on the screen from a program the PRINT command must be used. Anything following the PRINT statement, which is enclosed in inverted commas, will be printed on the screen. Therefore, if the line

```
PRINT "What is your name"
```

was included in a program, 'What is your name' would appear in the top left corner of the screen.

The TAB statement

The position of the printing on the screen can be controlled by adding the TAB statement. The origin for text is at the top left corner of the screen, and the number of characters which can be placed across and down depends on which MODE is being used. All the graphics MODES, that is MODES 0,1,2,4 and 5, can have 32 characters down the screen, and MODES 0 and 1 have 80 and 40 characters across respectively.

The following short program would place the word 'HELLO' in the centre of the screen in MODE 1:

```
10 MODE 1
20 PRINT TAB(18,16) "HELLO"
```

The next program produces an interesting pattern on the screen.

The basic pattern is obtained by drawing straight lines across a square in a stepped sequence. Try to work out how the MOVE and DRAW statements in lines 40, 50, 60 and 70 control the drawing to produce the pattern. The interesting 'interference' patterns are obtained by using the GCOL command in line 20, which specifies how the colour is placed on the screen. A full explanation of this command is beyond the scope of this book, but can be looked up in any one of a number of books dealing with the BBC micro. Enter this program and run it.

```
10 MODE 1
20 GCOL0,3
30 FOR P=0 TO 1023 STEP 12
40 MOVE P+128,0
50 DRAW (1023-P)+128,1023
60 MOVE 128,P
70 DRAW 1023+128,1023-P
80 NEXT P
```

If you now add the following line and re-run the program you will see how the program can be used to produce personalised patterns containing a name or any other message:

```
90 PRINT TAB(16,15)"MY NAME"
```

The lettering is improved if the following lines are used:

```
 90 VDU 5
100 GCOL0,0
110 MOVE 600,600
120 PRINT "MY"
130 MOVE 575,500
140 PRINT "NAME"
```

The VDU 5 command combines the **text cursor** with the **graphics cursor**, so that we can use the same co-ordinate system for positioning text as we have used for graphics. This gives finer control of text position.

The GCOL statement in line 100 allows white print to appear on the black background rather than the black print in a white rectangle, as in the previous example. If you would like to obtain a print of this pattern on an Epson printer you can add a command in line 150 if there is a suitable **screen dump ROM** fitted to the computer.

The illustration (Figure 2.6, page 8) and listing given demonstrate the use of this program with a **graphics dump ROM**.

```
 10 MODE 1
 20 GCOL0,3
 30 FOR P=0 TO 1023 STEP 12
 40 MOVE P+128,0
 50 DRAW(1023-P)+128,1023
 60 MOVE 128,P
 70 DRAW 1023+128,1023-P
 80 NEXT P
 90 VDU 5
100 GCOL0,0
110 MOVE 600,600
120 PRINT "MY"
130 MOVE 575,500
140 PRINT "NAME"
150 *GDUMP
```

Figure 2.6

Broken lines

Most drawing requires that you produce a variety of lines, like centre lines and dotted lines. A dotted line can be produced using the PLOT 21,X,Y command.

Clear the screen and enter this short program:

```
10 MODE 0
20 MOVE 0,512
30 PLOT 21,1280,512
```

This will draw a dotted line across the screen.

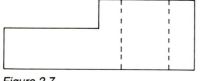

Figure 2.7

Exercise

The following program will draw the outline shown in Figure 2.7. Enter the program and RUN it. Modify the program so that the dotted lines are included in the drawing on the screen.

```
10 MODE 1
20 MOVE 200,200
30 DRAW 1000,200
40 DRAW 1000,500
50 DRAW 600,500
60 DRAW 600,350
70 DRAW 200,350
80 DRAW 200,200
```

'State of the art' computer graphics

A computer-generated shaded picture of the Rover 800 (see page 2)

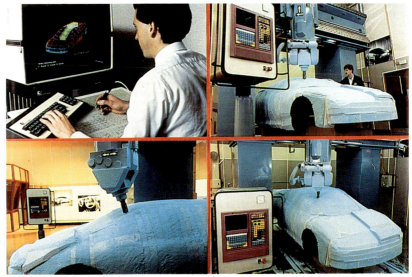

A computer-controlled model-making machine cutting a model from the CAD image (see page 2)

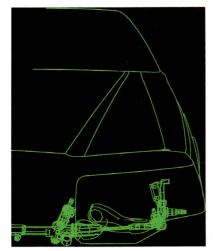

Three images produced using computer systems (see page 1)

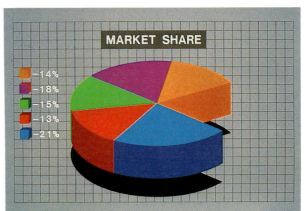

Computer images from Electronic Arts Ltd (see page 1)

A three-dimensional image of a car body from Computervision (see pages 1 and 2)

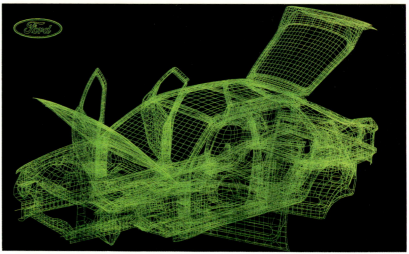

Computer drawings used for car design at the Ford Motor Company (see pages 1 and 2)

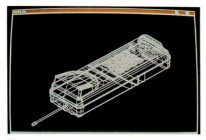

Three computer images from PA Design showing the use of CAD in product design (see pages 1 and 2)

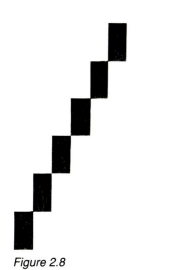

Figure 2.8

Pixel size and resolution

All the lines we have drawn so far have been horizontal or vertical, and in these circumstances the effect of the pixel size does not show clearly. When sloping lines are drawn, the benefit of higher resolution can really be appreciated. Enter the following program and RUN it. If you look closely you will see that the sloping line is not a straight line at all, but a series of small steps, as indicated in Figure 2.8. Remember to press the [RETURN] key after each line.

```
10 MODE 0
20 MOVE 200,300
30 DRAW 600,700
```

List the program again and re-type line 10 as follows:

```
10 MODE 2
```

After pressing [RETURN], the computer will replace the old line 10 with the last one typed. To prove this for yourself type L.[RETURN] and look at the new listing which appears.

Now RUN the program. You should clearly see the difference in the steps created by the pixels, which are larger in MODE 2. This is the reason we will use MODE 0 for most of our graphics. We are more concerned with the line quality at the moment than colour or memory available in the computer.

Before proceeding with the exercises below we will summarise the **BASIC** commands used so far for producing graphics.

MODE   places the computer into a mode specified by the number following the command. This number can be in the range 0 to 7, but must be 0,1,2,4 or 5 for graphics. MODE 0 gives the graphics of the highest resolution.

PLOT 69,X,Y   illuminates a point at the co-ordinates given by X,Y.

MOVE X,Y   moves the graphics cursor to the point given by the co-ordinates X,Y.

DRAW X,Y   draws a line from the last position of the cursor to the point given by the co-ordinates X and Y following the DRAW statement.

CLS   clears the screen.

LIST or L.   lists a program.

Exercises

1. Prepare a program to draw a line from the origin to the top right corner of the screen.
2. Write a program to reproduce pattern (a) on the screen.
3. Write programs to reproduce shapes (b) and (c). One side of each figure has been given a dimension in screen co-ordinate units. You should make up the rest to reproduce the figures on the screen in the same proportions to those given.

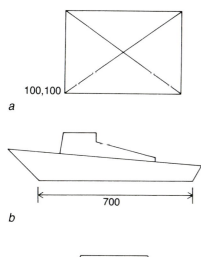

a   100,100

b   700

c   600

Using a screen grid

The following listing places a grid on the screen. Enter it into the computer and RUN it to see the grid.

```
10 MODE 0
20 Y=10
30 REPEAT
40 FOR X=0 TO 1280 STEP 100
50 PLOT 69,X,Y
60 NEXT X
70 Y=Y+100
80 UNTIL Y>1024
```

The program is quite simple and uses the PLOT 69 command, which we have already used, to plot a point on the screen. The Y value is set to 10 in line 20 and the X value is set to move across the screen in steps of 100 screen units by the FOR – NEXT loop in lines 40 and 60. The Y value is increased by 100 in line 70 and another row of points is illuminated across the screen. This process is repeated by the REPEAT – UNTIL loop in lines 30 and 80 until the Y value reaches 1024, which is the top of the screen.

This grid is now incorporated into program 2.1 which will help you write programs to construct various shapes on the screen.

Here is a summary of what some of the keys on the keyboard are programmed to do:

- G displays the grid.
- C will erase the grid.
- Pressing the red key f0 will enable you to program the shapes using line numbers between 10 and 1000.
- Pressing the red key f1 will get the computer to draw the image you have programmed.

Programming techniques are used which we have not yet discussed, but it is not important for you to understand how these work at the moment.

Enter program 2.1 into the computer and RUN it. Press the red key f0 and enter the following lines:

```
10 MOVE 200,300
20 DRAW 200,500
30 DRAW 1000,500
40 DRAW 1000,300
50 DRAW 200,300
```

Now press the red key f1 and you will see that we have programmed a rectangle to appear in the centre of the screen.

You can program drawing commands into program 2.1 by using line numbers 10 to 1000 after pressing the red key f0. Make sure you do not use line numbers above 1000 for drawing instructions as this would interfere with the grid drawing part of the program.

Program 2.1

```
1 *KEY0*FX125|MCLS|MLIST10,1000|M
2 *KEY1RUN|M
3 MODE0
4 VDU23,1,0;0;0;0;
5 REPEAT
6 X$=INKEY$(0)
7 IF X$="G" THEN PROCgrid
8 IF X$="C" THEN PROCerase
9 VDU28,0,15,20,0
```

```
1010 UNTIL X$="F"
1020 END
1030 DEFPROCgrid
1040 Y=0
1050 REPEAT
1060 FOR X=0 TO 1280 STEP 100
1070 PLOT69,X,Y
1080 NEXT X
1090 Y=Y+100
1100 UNTIL Y>1024
1110 ENDPROC
1120 DEFPROCerase
1130 Y=0
1140 REPEAT
1150 FOR X=0 TO 1280 STEP 100
1160 PLOT71,X,Y
1170 NEXT X
1180 Y=Y+100
1190 UNTIL Y>1024
1200 ENDPROC
```

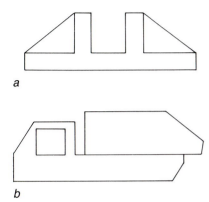

a

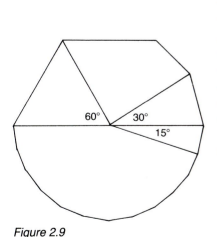

b

Exercises

1 Use the screen grid program to reproduce on the screen shapes (a) and (b).
2 Make up some shapes of your own on paper and translate them into screen images by using the screen grid program.

Drawing curves

Computers are not very clever and need to be told how to do every stage of any problem. The process of producing graphics is no exception. Commands in BBC BASIC like MOVE and DRAW provide shortcuts for drawing straight lines, but the computer needs mathematical formulae to calculate points on a curve which are then drawn by joining up adjacent points with straight lines. This leads to curves appearing a little false as they are really a series of straight lines.

Drawing circles

To see how curves are constructed by the computer we will look closely at how circles are drawn. The formulae and programs presented can be used even though you may not understand the mathematics involved. One of the most common ways of getting a computer to draw a circle is to treat the circle as a polygon with so many sides that it takes on the appearance of a circle. Figure 2.9 demonstrates this idea.

The trigonometry involved is explained briefly here, but you may need to seek help from your teachers to understand it thoroughly.

In any right-angled triangle the ratio of the sides give trigonometric values, for example, sin, cos, which can be used to calculate unknown lengths or angles. These values can be found in trigonometric tables or by using calculators with these functions or, of course, by using a computer. Figure 2.10 (page 14) shows these ratios.

When asking the computer to draw a circle we will know the radius required, and the angle will increase from 0 to 360 degrees in steps which will dictate the polygon drawn. For example, steps of 60 degrees will give a hexagon, whereas steps of 10 degrees will give a good approximation of a circle (Figure 2.11, page 14).

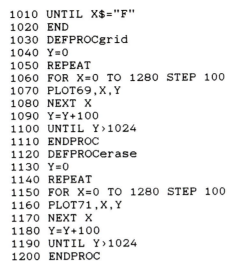

Figure 2.9

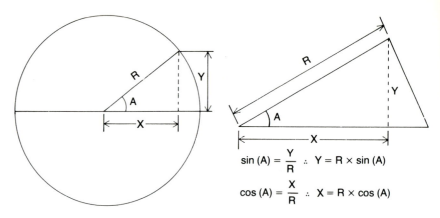

$\sin(A) = \dfrac{Y}{R} \therefore Y = R \times \sin(A)$

$\cos(A) = \dfrac{X}{R} \therefore X = R \times \cos(A)$

Figure 2.10

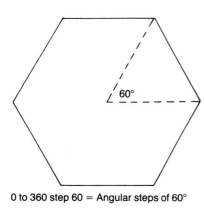

0 to 360 step 60 = Angular steps of 60°

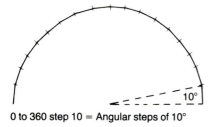

0 to 360 step 10 = Angular steps of 10°

Figure 2.11

Whether you have understood the mathematics involved or not, the important thing is to be able to use the formulae we get to draw a circle. These formulae, which can be used to calculate any point on the circle, are

$X = R \times \cos(\text{angle})$
$Y = R \times \sin(\text{angle})$

Here is a simple program to draw a circle:

```
10 MODE 0
20 R=200
30 VDU 29,640;512;
40 MOVE R,0
50 FOR angle=0 TO 360 STEP 10
60 A=RAD(angle)
70 DRAW R*COS(A),R*SIN(A)
80 NEXT
```

RUN the program, then LIST the program and make the following alteration:

```
60 FOR angle=0 TO 360 STEP 60
```

Re-RUN the program and you will clearly see that the program draws a polygon, and by increasing the number of steps (by making the angular steps in line 60 smaller) the polygon can take on the appearance of a circle. Any increase above about 40 steps will cease to improve the quality of the circle as the resolution of the screen image cannot cope with finer steps.

Here is an explanation of the program lines.

10 Sets the MODE.
20 Sets the radius of the circle to 200 units.
30 Defines the centre of the screen as the graphics origin (that is, the centre of the circle). The VDU 29,X;Y; command tells the computer to make the graphics origin at the position given by the co-ordinates X and Y.
40 Moves the cursor to the first point on the circumference of the circle.
50 Sets the angle step size. Here there will be 36 steps, which is about the best resolution we can expect using this system.
60 Converts the angle from degrees to radians. This is necessary because the computer cannot work with angles given in degrees but has to work in radians. A radian is approximately 57 degrees,

but the computer will convert angles in degrees to radians and this is being done by this line of the program.

- 70 Draws a line from the last position of the cursor to the new co-ordinates.
- 80 Makes the computer go back to line 50 to repeat the process for the next angular step. Lines 50 and 80, with the FOR – NEXT statements, form a loop which is repeated until all the steps have been worked out and drawn. In this case the angle increases by 10 degrees each time until it reaches 360 degrees.

We can modify the program slightly to make it more versatile and interactive. Make the following modifications to the program:

```
15 PRINT:PRINT
20 INPUT "RADIUS";R
```

These modifications are explained here:

- 15 Tells the computer to print two blank lines, and this makes sure the instruction in line 20 is not squashed up against the top of the screen.
- 20 Tells the computer to expect an input and the value of that input will be stored and named R. In other words, the computer will know that R = the value of the input we give it. Anything placed in inverted commas after the INPUT statement will be printed on the screen. This is to help us understand what the computer wants. In this case we have to enter the RADIUS of the circle. You should be able to work out the maximum value that can be entered before the circle will disappear off the screen.

At the moment the program runs through and then ends. We can make it a little more interesting by modifying it so that we have the option to repeat the program. Add the following lines:

```
 90 PRINT "PRESS R TO REPEAT"
100 key=GET
110 REPEAT
120 UNTIL key=&52
130 GOTO 20
```

The additional lines have the following effect on the program:

- 90 Prints the instruction on the screen to press the R key to repeat the program.
- 100 Tells the computer to wait for a key to be pressed. When a key is pressed the variable 'key' will be given the value of the **ASCII** (American Standard Code for Information Interchange) code number for the key which has been pressed.
- 110 Sets up a repeat loop, along with line 120, that waits for the R key to be pressed. In line 120 & 52 is the **hexadecimal** ASCII code number for the letter R.
- 130 Once the R key has been pressed the program continues, and this line sends the computer back to line 20. If you would like the screen cleared every time the program is repeated, change line 130 to GOTO 10.

Exercise

Modify the program so that the co-ordinates for the centre of the circle can be input by the user (use VDU 29,X;Y;).

Drawing filled circles

Filled circles can be drawn using the PLOT 85 command which produces filled triangles. We have seen that the computer constructs circles by drawing a series of triangular shapes. If each of these triangles is filled as it is drawn, the result will be a filled circle. The following program demonstrates this technique.

```
10 MODE 1
20 R=200
30 VDU 29,640;512;
40 MOVE R,0
50 FOR angle=0 TO 360
60 A=RAD(angle)
70 MOVE 0,0
80 PLOT 85,R*COS(A),R*SIN(A)
90 NEXT
```

The drawing of a circle has been discussed in some depth so that you can appreciate how difficult it can be to get a computer to draw the simplest of curves. We will be using other curves in the book but we will not be looking at the understanding of the mathematical formulae used to get those curves. We will use them as a means to obtaining computer graphics which can be used for design inspiration and assistance with design development.

Here is a short program which draws another type of curve called a sine wave.

```
10 MODE 0
20 MOVE 0,512
30 FOR X=0 TO 1200 STEP 4
40 DRAW X,512*(1+SIN(X/100))
50 NEXT X
```

Drawing ellipses

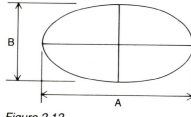

Figure 2.12

The equation for an ellipse is similar to that for a circle:

$X = A \times \cos(\text{angle})$
$Y = B \times \sin(\text{angle})$

A and B are the lengths of the major and minor axes, as shown in Figure 2.12.

The following short program will draw an ellipse in the centre of the screen:

```
10 MODE 0
20 VDU 29,640;512;
30 A=300:B=150
40 MOVE 0,150
50 FOR angle=0 TO 360 STEP 10
60 ANGLE=RAD(angle)
70 DRAW A*SIN(ANGLE),B*COS(ANGLE)
80 NEXT angle
```

Exercises

1. Write a program to draw an ellipse in the centre of the screen with the long axis running vertically.
2. Modify the program so that the computer asks for the X and Y co-ordinates for the centre of the ellipse and then draws the ellipse at those co-ordinates.

2.3 The use of PROCEDURES in drawing

This is a suitable point to introduce a feature of BBC BASIC which makes the structuring of programs much easier. We have already encountered the PROCEDURE feature in the earlier grid program. With other forms of BASIC, sub-routines have to be used which are not as versatile as the PROCEDURE facility offered by the BBC microcomputer. Programs can be put together containing PROCEDURES which can be called from the main program. The command for calling a PROCEDURE is PROC, followed by the name given to the procedure — for example, PROCexample would be the call line for a PROCEDURE called example. The procedure would be defined in lines following one containing the command DEF PROCexample. A procedure to draw an ellipse could be called by PROCellipse and program 2.2 demonstrates its use.

Program 2.2

```
10 MODE0
20 VDU29,620;512;
30 PROCellipse
40 END
50 DEF PROCellipse
60 A=300:B=150
70 MOVE0,150
80 FOR angle=0 TO 360 STEP 10
90 ANGLE=RAD(angle)
100 DRAW A*SIN(ANGLE),B*COS(ANGLE)
110 NEXT
120 ENDPROC
```

Note that the PROCEDURE has to end with the command ENDPROC and the end of the main program has to be identified with the END statement in line 40 in order to separate the main program from the PROCEDURES. Another useful feature of the PROCEDURE facility is that variables can be carried into the PROCEDURE from the call line. Therefore, PROCellipse(400,200) would carry the values 400 and 200 into an ellipse drawing procedure which could begin with the line DEF PROCellipse (XC,YC). This enables us to draw ellipses of different sizes using one PROCEDURE. This facility is also useful if the graphics origin needs to be defined several times within a program. The call could be PROCorigin(300,200) and the PROCEDURE could be DEF PROCorigin (X,Y). This would define the graphics origin at the point (300,200).

The use of the PROCEDURE is demonstrated in program 2.3, which draws a cylinder on the screen. This drawing requires two ellipses with the associated redefining of the graphics origin. Without the PROCEDURE facility the program would become much longer.

Program 2.3

```
 10 MODE0
 20 PROCorigin(640,800)
 30 PROCellipse(300,130)
 40 PROCorigin(640,200)
 50 PROCellipse(300,130)
 60 VDU29,0;0;
 70 MOVE 940,200
 80 DRAW 940,800
 90 MOVE 340,200
100 DRAW 340,800
110 END
120 ENDPROC
200 DEF PROCorigin(X,Y)
210 VDU29,X;Y;
220 ENDPROC
300 DEF PROCellipse(XC,YC)
310 MOVE 0,YC
320 FOR angle=0 TO 360 STEP 10
330 ANGLE=RAD(angle)
340 DRAW XC*SIN(ANGLE),YC*COS(ANGLE)
350 NEXT
360 ENDPROC
```

Exercise

Modify program 2.3 to draw a cylinder with the axis running horizontally.

The use of the PROCEDURE, in graphics, can be further demonstrated when the drawing of a number of rectangles is required. A rectangle can be drawn on the computer using the following format (Figure 2.13):

```
10 MODE 0
20 X=300:Y=400:W=400:H=500
30 MOVE X,Y
40 DRAW X+W,Y
50 DRAW X+W,Y+H
60 DRAW X,Y+H
70 DRAW X,Y
```

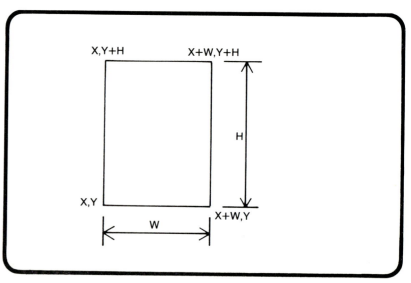

Figure 2.13

This form is now adapted to produce two rectangles by carrying values into the PROCEDURE from the call line in line 40. Program 2.4 also shows how the DATA and READ commands can be used to read data from a list at the end of the program. In this way many values can be read into the PROCEDURE call in line 40. The READ statement causes the computer to place the values, which it reads from the DATA lines, into the variables X,Y,W and H in line 30. These values are then used in line 40 to be taken into the PROCEDURE for drawing the rectangle. The READ − UNTIL X=−1 loop in lines 30 and 50 causes the READ instruction to continue until the value −1 is read, when the program will end. Note how the DATA lines are presented, for example:

```
170 DATA 100,200,400,500
```

Each number replaces X,Y,W and H respectively in the READ command at line 30.

Program 2.4

```
 10 MODE0
 20 REPEAT
 30 READ X,Y,W,H
 40 PROCbox(X,Y,W,H)
 50 UNTIL X=-1
 60 END
 70 MOVE 940,200
 80 DRAW 940,800
 90 MOVE 340,200
100 DEFPROCbox(X,Y,W,H)
110 MOVE X,Y
120 DRAW X+W,Y
130 DRAW X+W,Y+H
140 DRAW X,Y+H
150 DRAW X,Y
160 ENDPROC
170 DATA 100,200,400,500
180 DATA 800,200,400,500
190 DATA -1,-1,-1,-1,-1
```

Exercise
Using the rectangle drawing PROCEDURE given above, write a program to draw an image similar to the one shown on the left.

2.4 User-defined graphics

Each letter, number or other character is made up of a pattern of pixels within an 8 × 8 grid as demonstrated in Figure 2.14.

Most computers offer the facility for the user to create a series of characters. These user-defined characters are particularly useful for games but can also be utilised in other situations. Each of the characters contained in the computer has an ASCII (American Standard Code for Information Interchange) code number. The computer's standard character set contains all the characters necessary for the alphabet, numbers and all the other symbols found on the keyboard.

Enter the following into the computer and observe what happens:

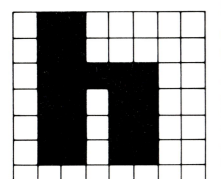

Figure 2.14

```
PRINT CHR$(35)
```

Try some other numbers between 32 and 126 in the brackets.

If you wish to define your own characters or shapes on the BBC computer, then ASCII codes 224 to 255, inclusive, are left available for this purpose. The VDU 23 code is used to define these characters. An 8 × 8 grid is drawn and the user's shape is planned within it. Each vertical column is allocated a number, as indicated in Figure 2.15. The numeric value for each horizontal row results from adding these column values for each pixel that is to be illuminated in that row.

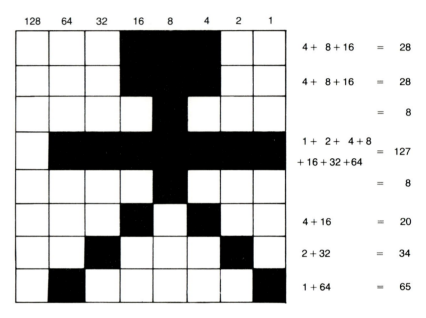

Figure 2.15

The character illustrated in Figure 2.13 would be defined as follows:

```
VDU 23,224,28,28,8,127,8,20,34,65
```

The number (224) following the VDU 23 code is the ASCII number given to this particular shape, and the following numbers are the totals for each of the horizontal rows, running from top to bottom. Note that adding any columns together will always produce a unique number so that, for example, 28 can only result in blocks 16, 8 and 4 being illuminated.

The following short program will print the defined character on the screen:

```
10 MODE 1
20 VDU 23,224,28,28,8,127,8,20,34,65
30 PRINT TAB(10,10) CHR$(224)
```

The character shown in Figure 2.16 will be used as a graphics cursor in Chapter 4.

Figure 2.16

This character is defined as follows:

```
VDU 23,230,24,24,60,231,231,60,24,24
```

Exercise

Draw an 8 × 8 grid on a piece of paper and design some characters of your own. Devise programs to print them on the screen.

Figures can be made to appear to move by drawing and erasing slightly altered forms of the same character. The following program demonstrates this technique.

Program 2.5

```
 10 MODE 2
 20 VDU23,224,28,28,8,127,8,20,34,65
 30 VDU23,225,93,62,28,8,8,20,20,20
 40 VDU 5
 50 MOVE 640,512
 60 VDU 224
 70 FOR T=1 TO 500:NEXT
 80 VDU 127
 90 VDU 225
100 FOR T=1 TO 500:NEXT
110 VDU 127
120 GOTO 50
```

This program is run in MODE 2 so that the character is bigger. It also introduces another system for printing the character. The VDU 5 command in line 40 combines the text cursor with the graphics cursor so that the graphics screen co-ordinates can be used. The VDU statements in lines 60 and 90 are another way of printing defined characters on the screen. The VDU 127 command in lines 80 and 110 automatically backspaces and deletes the character on the screen so that the other version may be drawn.

You might like to try moving characters around on the screen by making the following alterations to the program:

```
 45 X=10:Y=500
 50 MOVE X,Y
115 X=X+20
```

The characters we have defined as 224 and 225 do not suit this sort of movement, and you might like to design some of your own. Draw out an 8 × 8 grid to plan some suitable shapes and try writing short programs which produce moving figures.

There are many more techniques associated with user-defined characters, but it is not within the scope of this book to deal with this aspect of computer graphics in any more detail. There are many books available which cover this topic in more depth.

3 Creative patterns

3.1 Geometric patterns

The computer can calculate solutions to geometric equations very quickly, which means that it can be programmed to draw a variety of geometric shapes far more quickly than by using manual drawing methods. The ideas presented in this section can be used to generate a variety of patterns which can be printed out (or copied from the screen), to be kept in a design scrapbook which will act as a reference resource for future design work. It is useful to keep sketchbooks of things from a variety of sources (natural forms, textures, structures and so on), to act as a source of inspiration and build up a store of visual images to help with design projects. The patterns generated by computers can be added to such a collection.

A printed copy of the screen images can be obtained using several output devices. The program given here can be used with a dot-matrix printer, an MCP 40 type plotter (page vii) or a Plotmate plotter, and you should be able to use at least one of them.

If there are no facilities for obtaining a printed copy of the screen

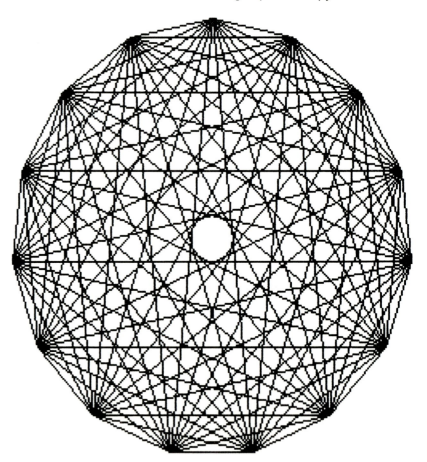

Figure 3.1

images, layout paper (or tracing paper), can be taped to the screen and the patterns can be copied by tracing them on to the paper using a soft pencil.

Most of the equations used for producing the geometric figures are quite complex but we can use the programs for our purposes without concerning ourselves with a detailed understanding of the mathematics involved, and mathematical details will be used only as a means to achieving the end result.

The following listing produces an interesting geometric pattern which can be modified by the user, who has control of the number of sides the basic figure will have.

Program 3.1

```
10 MODE0
20 DIMX(20):DIMY(20)
30 PRINT:PRINT
40 INPUT"INPUT THE NUMBER OF SIDES(3 TO 20)",N
50 IF N<3 OR N>20 GOTO 20
60 FOR P=0 TO N-1
70 X(P)=600+500*SIN(P*2*PI/N)
80 Y(P)=500+500*COS(P*2*PI/N)
90 NEXT:CLS
100 FOR J=1 TO N/2
110 FOR P=0 TO N-1
120 MOVE X(P),Y(P)
130 K=(P+J) MOD N
140 DRAW X(K),Y(K)
150 NEXT:NEXT
```

From N. Holmes in Electronic and Computing Monthly, *March 1985.*

The print-out shown in Figure 3.1 was obtained on an Epson **dot matrix printer**, using a Computer Concepts Printmaster **ROM**. The ROM command for the screen dump is added to the program as follows:

```
160 *GDUMP
```

Other ROMs can be used and their appropriate command placed in line 160.

If the following lines are added to the previous program the image can be plotted out on an MCP 40-type plotter. Figure 3.2 (page 24) shows an example done on this type of plotter.

```
160 PRINT"PRESS R TO REPEAT"
170 PRINT"PRESS P TO PRINT"
180 PRINT"PRESS Q TO QUIT"
190 command$=GET$
200 IF command$="R" THEN 25
210 IF command$="P" THEN 240
220 IF command$="Q" THEN CLS:PRINT TAB(5,15)
        "THE PROGRAM HAS NOW FINISHED":END
230 GOTO 190
240 VDU 2
250 VDU1,18
260 FORP=0 TO N-1
270 X(P)=200+180*SIN(P*2*PI/N)
280 Y(P)=180+180*COS(P*2*PI/N)
290 NEXT
300 FORJ=1 TO N/2
310 FORP=0 TO N-1
320 PRINT"M"+STR$X(P)+","+STR$Y(P)
```

```
330 K=(P+J) MOD N
340 PRINT"D"+STR$(X(K)+","+STR$Y(K)
350 NEXT:NEXT
360 PRINT"A"
370 VDU 3
380 GOTO 25
```

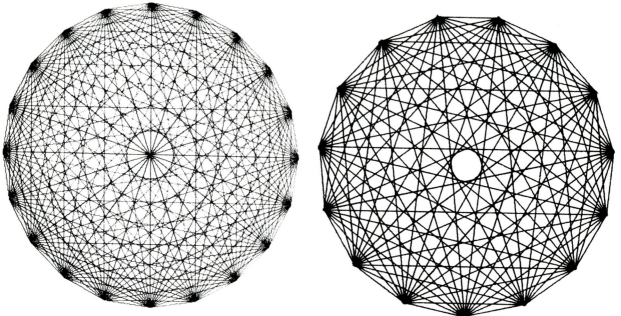

Figure 3.2

Figure 3.3

Program 3.2 is a modification of the previous listing, so that the pattern may be drawn out on a Plotmate plotter. The additional lines in the program call up operating procedures from 'the Plotmate ROM', and a full explanation of this technique can be found in section 2 of the Plotmate manual, under the heading 'Plotting from Programs'. Figure 3.3 shows a plotter image produced using program 3.2.

Line 250 is the code to control the scale of the drawing produced on the Plotmate. The last number in the row is the scaling number and can take a value in the range 1 to 255. Try altering the number 50 in line 260 and see the effect it has on the plotted image.

Program 3.2

```
10 MODE0
20 DIMX(20):DIMY(20)
30 PRINT:PRINT
40 INPUT"INPUT THE NUMBER OF SIDES(3 TO 20)",N
50 IF N<3 OR N>20 GOTO 20
60 FOR P=0 TO N-1
70 X(P)=600+500*SIN(P*2*PI/N)
80 Y(P)=500+500*COS(P*2*PI/N)
90 NEXT:CLS
100 FOR J=1 TO N/2
110 FOR P=0 TO N-1
120 MOVE X(P),Y(P)
130 K=(P+J) MOD N
140 DRAW X(K),Y(K)
150 NEXT:NEXT
```

```
160 PRINT "DO YOU WANT A PRINT Y/N"
170 KEY=GET
180 IF KEY=89 THEN PROCplot
190 IF KEY=78 THEN PROCclear
200 GOTO 170
210 DEF PROCplot
220 *PLTMATE
230 *ONMATE
240 MOVE 200,200
250 VDU23,255,0,0,0,0,0,1,0,50
260 GOTO 60
270 ENDPROC
280 DEF PROCclear
290 *HOME
300 *OFFMATE
310 CLS:GOTO 30
320 ENDPROC
```

3.2 Polygon patterns

We have already seen how the computer draws polygons in Chapter 2, when we used a polygon with many sides to represent a circle. Program 3.3 will draw a pattern based on the rotation of a polygon whilst it gradually gets smaller.

Program 3.3

```
 10 MODE1
 20 D=30:R=500
 30 FOR T=1 TO 35
 40 PROCpoly(640,512,R,R,6,D)
 50 D=D+5:R=R*0.95
 60 NEXT T
 70 REM *GDUMP HERE
 80 END
 90 DEF PROCpoly(XC,YC,XR,YR,N,D)
100 PROCorigin(XC,YC)
110 A=2*PI/N:DR=D*PI/180
120 MOVE XR*COS(DR),YR*SIN(DR)
130 FOR P=1 TO N
140 X=XR*COS(P*A+DR)
150 Y=YR*SIN(P*A+DR)
160 DRAW X,Y
170 NEXT P
180 ENDPROC
190 DEFPROCorigin(XC,YC)
200 VDU 29,XC;YC;
210 ENDPROC
```

This form of the program draws a hexagon and rotates it 35 times, each one getting smaller. The number of sides in the polygon is fixed to six in the values following the PROCpoly call and the diameter of the base circle for the polygon and the angular steps used are fixed in line 20. The first two values (in brackets), after the PROCpoly call, are the values for a new graphics origin (640,512) to be used in the PROCorigin call. The brackets also contain the radius (R), number of sides (N) and angular rotation (D) used to draw the polygon. These values are carried into the procedure in line 90. The REM statement in line 70 is short for REMARK and is ignored by the computer. It provides the user with information and is used here to show where the screen dump ROM command should be placed.

Exercise

Modify program 3.3 so that it draws a pattern based on an octagon which is revolved and drawn 30 times.

Program 3.4 extends the listing of program 3.3 to make it interactive. When you run the program, the computer will request you to input the number of sides and revolutions required, and after drawing the pattern you will have the option of obtaining a print of the pattern or inputting new information for another pattern. The lines from 200 dump the image to the MCP 40 plotter, but the appropriate screen dump ROM command can be placed in line 210 for a dump to a dot matrix printer.

Program 3.5 is the same program, but modified so that the screen image can be drawn out on a Plotmate plotter. Figures 3.4 to 3.6 show some of the patterns obtained with programs 3.4 and 3.5.

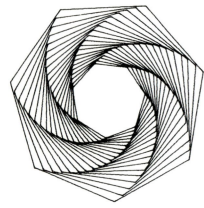

Figure 3.4

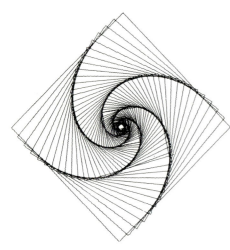

Figure 3.5

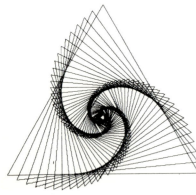

Figure 3.6

Program 3.4

```
10 REM MULTIPLE POLYGON PROGRAM WITH TANDY
            PLOTTER DUMP
20 MODE0
30 D=30:R=400
40 INPUT"NUMBER OF SIDES",N
50 INPUT"NUMBER OF REVOLUTIONS",T
60 FOR K=1 TO T
70 PROCpoly(640,430,R,R,N,D)
80 D=D+5:R=R*0.95
90 NEXT K
100 PRINT"PRESS P FOR A PRINT"
110 PRINT"PRESS Q FOR ANOTHER PATTERN"
120 command$=GET$
130 IF command$="P" THEN PROCprint
140 IF command$="Q" THEN 20
150 GOTO 120
160 END
170 DEF PROCpoly(XC,YC,XR,YR,N,D)
180 PROCorigin(XC,YC)
190 A=2*PI/N:DR=D*PI/180
200 MOVE XR*COS(DR),YR*SIN(DR)
210 FOR P=1 TO N
220 X=XR*COS(P*A+DR)
230 Y=YR*SIN(P*A+DR)
240 DRAW X,Y
250 NEXT P
260 ENDPROC
270 DEFPROCorigin(XC,YC)
280 VDU 29,XC;YC;
290 ENDPROC
300 DEF PROCprint
310 VDU2
320 VDU1,18
330 D=30:R=225
340 PRINT"M240,0":PRINT"I"
350 FOR K=1 TO T
360 A=2*PI/N:DR=D*PI/180
370 PRINT"M"+STR$(R*COS(DR))+","+STR$(R*SIN(DR))
380 GOSUB440
390 D=D+5:R=R*0.95
400 NEXT K
410 PRINT"A"
420 VDU3
430 CLS:GOTO30
440  FOR P=1 TO N
450 X=R*COS(P*A+DR)
```

Using programs in the text

Copper-wire filography produced using program 3.10 (page 36)

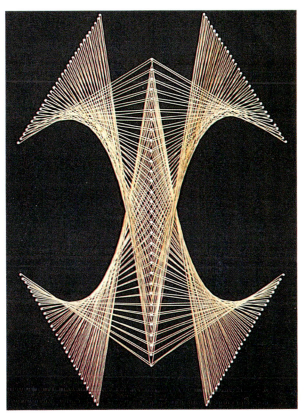

A more complex filographic pattern which could be produced with program 3.10 if it were suitably modified

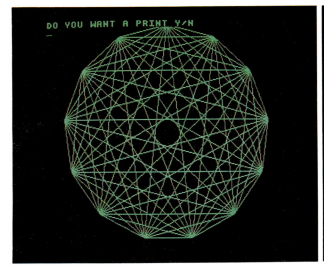

A screen shot from program 3.1 (page 23)

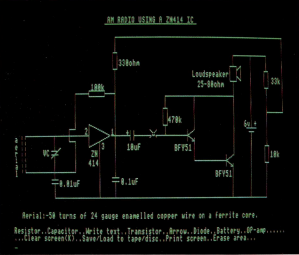

A screen shot from program 4.12 (pages 52–4)

Drawings showing the development of ideas for jewellery from computer patterns (see pages 30–33)

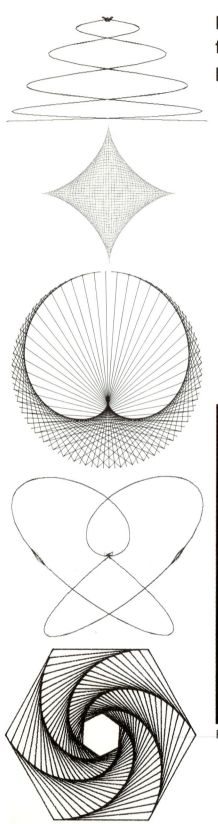

Pendants derived from computer patterns

Some computer-generated patterns

```
460 Y=R*SIN(P*A+DR)
470 PRINT"D"+STR$(X)+","+STR$(Y)
480 NEXT P
490 RETURN
```

Program 3.5

```
10 REM MULTIPLE POLYGON PROGRAM WITH PLOTMATE DUMP
20 MODE 0
30 INPUT"NUMBER OF SIDES",N
40 INPUT"NUMBER OF REVOLUTIONS",T
50 D=30:R=400
60 FOR K=1 TO T
70 PROCpoly(640,430,R,R,N,D)
80 D=D+5:R=R*0.95
90 NEXT K
100 PRINT"DO YOU WANT A PRINT Y/N"
110 KEY=GET
120 IF KEY=89 THEN PROCplot
130 IF KEY=78 THEN PROCclear
140 GOTO 110
150 END
160 DEF PROCpoly(XC,YC,XR,YR,N,D)
170 PROCorigin(XC,YC)
180 A=2*PI/N:DR=D*PI/180
190 MOVE XR*COS(DR),YR*SIN(DR)
200 FOR P=1 TO N
210 X=XR*COS(P*A+DR)
220 Y=YR*SIN(P*A+DR)
230 DRAW X,Y
240 NEXT P
250 ENDPROC
260 DEFPROCorigin(XC,YC)
270 VDU 29,XC;YC;
280 ENDPROC
290 DEF PROCplot
300 CLS
310 *PLTMATE
320 *ONMATE
330 VDU23,255,0,0,0,0,0,1,0,150
340 CLS
350 GOTO 50
360 ENDPROC
370 DEF PROCclear
380 *HOME
390 *OFFMATE
400 CLS:GOTO 30
410 ENDPROC
```

3.3 Lissajous patterns

The lissajous curve offers many possibilities for the creation of a variety of interesting and unusual patterns. This curve is drawn using similar formulae to those we have used for drawing a circle, which were:

$X = R \times \cos(\text{angle})$
$Y = R \times \sin(\text{angle})$

The system which uses an angle and a line length to calculate co-ordinates is called the 'polar co-ordinate system'. The circle is drawn by specifying a fixed length (R) and angles from 0 to 360 degrees, which are used to calculate X and Y co-ordinates for a number of points on the circle.

For a circle the value for 'angle' in the two equations should be the same. If the value of 'angle' is made different in the two equations the resulting curve will be a lissajous. The following program will demonstrate this principle.

```
10 MODE 0
20 VDU 29,640;512;
30 MOVE 200,0
40 FOR angle%=0 TO 900 STEP 2
50 angle=RAD(angle%)
60 DRAW 200*COS(angle*0.2),200*SIN(angle)
70 NEXT
```

Program 3.6 will produce a variety of basic lissajous patterns which are generated automatically. A new form can be started by pressing the space bar. Lines 80 and 110 set up a repeat loop which keeps drawing a particular pattern until the space bar is pressed. The command UNTIL INKEY (0)=32 tells the computer to look for a key being pressed, whose ASCII code number is 32. As we saw in Chapter 2, each key on the keyboard has a code number which is recognised by the computer, and the space bar has code number 32. Once the complete cycle of patterns has been completed, the program prompts you to press the space bar if you wish the sequence to be re-run.

Program 3.6

```
10 MODE0
20 VDU23;8202;0;0;0;
30 VDU29,640;512;
40 FOR S=0.2 TO 2.2 STEP 0.2
50 IF S›2 THEN PROCrepeat
60 MOVE 350,0
70 A=0
80 REPEAT
90 A=A+0.2
100 DRAW 350*COS(A*S),350*SIN(A)
110 UNTIL INKEY(0)=32
120 CLS
130 NEXT
140 DEF PROCrepeat
150 CLS:PRINT"ONE CYCLE HAS BEEN DEMONSTRATED"
160 PRINT"PRESS THE SPACE BAR TO RE-RUN
            THE SEQUENCE"
170 KEY=GET
180 IF KEY=32 THEN CLS:GOTO20
190 GOTO 170
```

Programs 3.7 and 3.8 use the lissajous curve in a more versatile way and offer a vast variety of patterns which can be used as a design resource. The programs are more interactive than the previous ones and allow greater flexibility for producing patterns. Program 3.7 is written with a dump routine for the MCP 40 plotter and program 3.8 contains a routine for the Plotmate plotter. Once program 3.8 has been entered into the computer, the Plotmate systems disk should be placed in the disk drive, as control routines contained on the disk are called from within the program.

On running the programs you will be asked to input any three variables. Three numbers are entered either by typing each number followed by the [RETURN] key, or by entering them thus:

13,3,13 [RETURN]

A pattern will then be generated and, once complete, a screen prompt will tell you how to obtain a print of the pattern.

In program 3.7, pressing P will give a plot on an MCP 40 type plotter, or the screen can be cleared by pressing R and the process repeated. The program contains a dump for the MCP 40 type plotter, but the PROCEDURE for the dump, which begins at line 190, can be modified for a dot matrix dump.

In program 3.8, once the pattern has been drawn on the screen the prompt

"DO YOU WANT A PRINT Y/N"

will appear. If the Plotmate systems disk is in the disk drive, pressing Y will produce a plot of the pattern.

Some of the patterns generated will prove to be of little use long before the computer has finished plotting them. To enable them to be interrupted, the break key has been defined to stop the program and re-run it. This is accomplished in line 10, where *KEY10 programs the the break key. Once the break key is pressed the program is interrupted, but it can be retrieved if the command OLD is entered into the computer. OLD¦M is the way of automatically entering the command OLD[RETURN] and RUN¦M automatically runs the program again. The ¦ symbol is found on the key next to the left-pointing cursor control key.

The values for angle, in line 60, can be set to vary between 0 and 360 degrees for some of the variables, but for many, it is best left at 180 degrees because a lot of over-drawing takes place. This results in a delay before the computer completes the pattern with no apparent drawing taking place.

The REM statement in line 70 indicates that the step size set in line 60 increases the speed at the cost of resolution as it is enlarged. The step of 0.5 is suitable for many of the variables, but as they get larger the step size needs to be reduced. It would be an improvement if you could modify the program to set the step size automatically to suit the variables input in line 40.

Examples of patterns produced using programs 3.7 and 3.8 are shown in Figures 3.7 to 3.11.

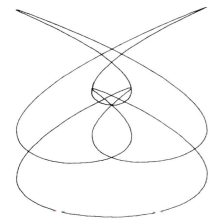

Figure 3.7 Variables 3,9,5

Figure 3.8 Variables 5,50,5

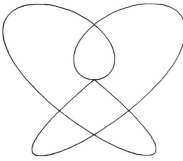

Figure 3.9 Variables 2,5,4; line 60 for angle = 0 to 360 STEP 0.5

Program 3.7

```
10  *KEY10 OLD¦MRUN¦M
20  MODE 0
30  xc=640:yc=512
40  INPUT"THREE VARIABLES",A%,B%,C%
50  VDU 29,xc;yc;
60  FOR angle=0 TO 180 STEP 0.5
70  REM For speed increase set step to 0.5, for
             better resolution 0.1
80  x=300*SIN(RAD(A%*angle))*COS(RAD(B%*angle))
90  y=300*SIN(RAD(A%*angle))*SIN(RAD(C%*angle))
100 IF angle=0 THEN MOVE x,y ELSE DRAW x,y
110 NEXT angle
```

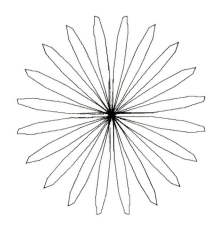

Figure 3.10 Variables 50,5,5

Figure 3.11 Variables 50,40,40

```
120 PRINT"PRESS P FOR A PRINT OUT"
130 PRINT"PRESS R TO DRAW ANOTHER PATTERN"
140 command$=GET$
150 IF command$="P" THEN PROCprint
160 IF command$="R" THEN CLS:GOTO30
170 GOTO140
180 DEF PROCprint
190 VDU2
200 VDU1,18
210 PRINT"M460,0":PRINT"I"
220 FOR angle=0 TO 360 STEP 0.25
230 x=300*SIN(RAD(A%*angle))*COS(RAD(B%*angle))
240 y=300*SIN(RAD(A%*angle))*SIN(RAD(C%*angle))
250 IF angle=0 THEN PRINT "M"+STR$(x)+",
        "+STR$(y) ELSE PRINT"D"+STR$(x)+","
        +STR$(y)
260 NEXT angle
270 PRINT"A"
280 VDU3
290 CLS
300 GOTO 30
```

Program 3.8

```
10 *KEY10 OLD¦MRUN¦M
20 MODE4
30 xc=640:yc=400
40 INPUT"THREE VARIABLES",A%,B%,C%
50 VDU 29,xc;yc;
60 FOR angle=0 TO 180 STEP 0.5
70 REM For speed increase step to 0.5, for
        better resolution 0.1
80 x=400*SIN(RAD(A%*angle))*COS(RAD(B%*angle))
90 y=400*SIN(RAD(A%*angle))*SIN(RAD(C%*angle))
100 IF angle=0 THEN MOVE x,y ELSE DRAW x,y
110 NEXT angle
120 PRINT"DO YOU WANT A PRINT Y/N"
130 KEY=GET
140 IF KEY=89 THEN PROCplot
150 IF KEY=78 THEN PROCclear
160 GOTO 130
170 DEF PROCplot
180 *PLTMATE
190 *ONMATE
200 VDU23,255,0,0,0,0,0,1,0,75
210 CLS
220 GOTO50
230 ENDPROC
240 DEF PROCclear
250 *HOME
260 *OFFMATE
270 CLS:GOTO 30
280 ENDPROC
```

3.4 Some applications for the pattern-generating programs

The variety of patterns which can be generated from the programs given in this section is extensive and you could modify the programs to use other geometric formulae for producing a greater selection. There are also many other programs which you could make up to do similar things. A variety of these patterns could be printed or plotted and kept in a design resource folder for future reference in your design work.

Many of the patterns obviously lend themselves to decorative applications, and with a little imagination and the use of an appropriate plotter, patterns could be drawn on acetate film and used to decorate a variety of projects, particularly those made in plastic. The plotter might be used to draw directly on to thin sheet plastic and the image 'fixed' with a light spraying of clear cellulose. It might also be possible to adapt some plotters to engrave into certain materials.

More specifically, the computer-generated patterns could be used to inspire ideas for new and interesting jewellery forms. In this context you will need to develop ideas originated by the computer using conventional methods of graphical communication. The illustrations on pages 27 and 28 show how items of jewellery could be derived from computer-generated patterns using a variety of materials to produce hand-drawn developments of the ideas.

Many original and unusual forms will result from some of the programs presented and this may inspire a fresh and original approach to certain problems concerning the development of form and decoration.

Finally, you might like to use your own imagination and inventiveness to develop some of the ideas presented here into other design and make situations. The very nature of CDT should encourage creativity and originality, and it is hoped that some of the ideas presented here will inspire alternative approaches to collecting design resource material and in searching for inspiration for new forms and patterns which can be used in your design work.

3.5 Recursion

'Recursion' is another word for repetition and is the term used to describe the repetition of a geometric shape to produce particular types of computer-generated patterns. Using this technique, many interesting and complex patterns can be produced. The basic process involves drawing a shape and then repeating that shape in other positions, with a scaling factor introduced so that the basic shape gets smaller.

Program 3.9 (page 34) demonstrates this principle using a square, and Figure 3.12 shows the output from the program. The technique relies on the fact that a procedure can be called from within itself with new variables carried from the call. The number of recursions that take place is controlled by the value in line 70. The calls to PROCsquare in lines 110,120,130 and 140 position a new square at each corner of the original one, and the value Z is halved each time. If the value in line 70 is Z<100, then clearly only two repeats will take place as Z was 200 to begin with. Perhaps you can predict what will happen if line 70 were

```
70 IF Z<50 THEN ENDPROC
```

List the program, change line 70 and re-run it. Figure 3.13 shows the new pattern that results.

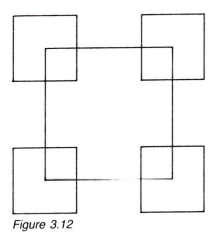

Figure 3.12

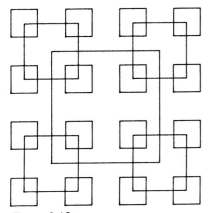

Figure 3.13

Program 3.9

```
10 MODE0
15 VDU23;8202;0;0;0
20 VDU5
40 PROCsquare(640,512,250)
70 END
80 DEF PROCsquare(X,Y,Z)
85 IF Z<100 THEN ENDPROC
90 VDU29,X;Y;
100 MOVEZ,Z
110 DRAWZ,-Z:DRAW-Z,-Z:DRAW-Z,Z:DRAWZ,Z
120 PROCsquare(X+Z,Y+Z,Z/2)
130 PROCsquare(X-Z,Y+Z,Z/2)
140 PROCsquare(X-Z,Y-Z,Z/2)
150 PROCsquare(X+Z,Y-Z,Z/2)
160 ENDPROC
```

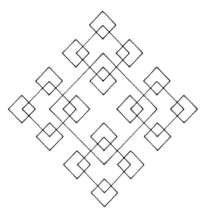

Figure 3.14

Try lower values in line 70.

In this type of program there are many interesting variations you can try. Program 3.9 can be modified to give the pattern shown in Figure 3.14. Make the following alterations to produce this pattern:

```
40 PROCdiamond(640,512,200)
60 DEFPROCdiamond(X,Y,Z)
100 MOVE Z,0
110 DRAW 0,Z:DRAW -Z,0:DRAW 0,-Z:DRAW Z,0
120 PROCdiamond(X+Z,Y,Z/2)
130 PROCdiamond(X-Z,Y,Z/2)
140 PROCdiamond(X,Y+Z,Z/2)
150 PROCdiamond(X,Y-Z,Z/2)
```

3.6 Filography

This is the name given to an art form where geometric patterns which look like curves are derived from straight lines. The work is usually produced by placing nails into a piece of board and weaving the pattern between the nails with thread or wire. The photographs on page 27 show examples of filographic pieces of art. The computer can quickly create ideas for patterns which might form the basis for such works of art.

Program 3.10 (page 36) is one that will enable you to create a variety of patterns which might be used for 'nail and thread' patterns. The program allows you to draw two lines, which can be divided into any number of equal divisions, which are then joined with straight lines.

Figure 3.15 shows how this principle works. The program allows you to decide how many divisions will be used, up to a maximum of 50, and to select the start and end point of each of the lines. The program will ask for the co-ordinates for the start and end of each of the lines. The following values should be used as an example to try the program. Each input should be entered by pressing the [RETURN] key.

- Number of points   20
- One end of first line   40,20
- Other end   500,1000
- One end of second line   1200,150
- Other end   600,1000

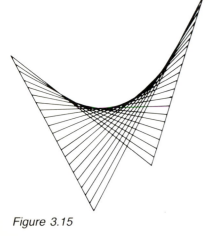

Figure 3.15

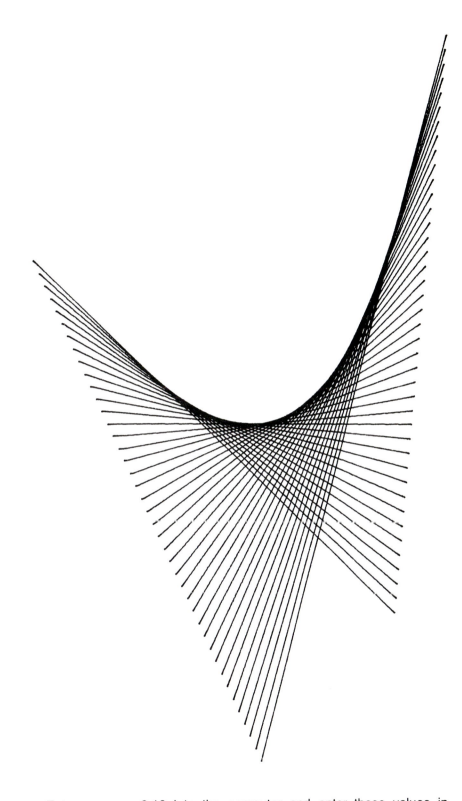

Figure 3.16

Enter program 3.10 into the computer and enter these values in response to the prompts given. You will see a **screen prompt** "ANOTHER PATTERN Y/N" appear once the pattern is complete. Press Y and enter your own values this time. Figure 3.16 illustrates a pattern produced with this program.

Program 3.10

```
 10 MODE 0
 20 VDU23;8202;0;0;0;
 30 DIM X1(50),Y1(50)
 40 DIM X2(50),Y2(50)
 50 INPUT "NUMBER OF POINTS",N
 60 INPUT"ONE END FIRST LINE"X1(0),Y1(0)
 70 INPUT"OTHER END",X1(N),Y1(N)
 80 INPUT"ONE END SECOND LINE"X2(0),Y2(0)
 90 INPUT"OTHER END",X2(N),Y2(N)
100 IX=(X1(N)-X1(0))/N:IY=(Y1(N)-Y1(0))/N
110 IX2=(X2(N)-X2(0))/N:IY2=(Y2(N)-Y2(0))/N
120 FOR T=1 TO N
130 X1(T)=X1(0)+(IX*T)
140 Y1(T)=Y1(0)+(IY*T)
150 X2(T)=X2(0)+(IX2*T)
160 Y2(T)=Y2(0)+(IY2*T)
170 NEXT T
180 Z=N
190 REPEAT
200 MOVE X1(Z-N),Y1(Z-N)
210 DRAW X2(N),Y2(N)
220 N=N-1
230 UNTIL N<0
240 PRINT"ANOTHER PATTERN Y/N"
250 KEY=GET
260 IF KEY=89 THEN CLEAR:GOTO10
270 IF KEY=78 THEN END
280 GOTO 250
```

Exercises

1 Re-write programs 3.9 or 3.10 so that more lines are used as the basis for the patterns produced, as indicated in Figure 3.17.
2 If you have a suitable printer or plotter available, modify the programs so that you can obtain a print of any chosen pattern.

If you would like to make a thread and nail picture of one of your patterns, you should take the plotted image or a screen tracing and lay it on an a piece of 12-mm chipboard of an appropriate size. A far better image results if the chipboard is first covered with a plain material such as crimplene or hessian. Small nails should be knocked into the board through all the division marks on the straight lines on the **plotout** or tracing. Once all the nails have been knocked in, the plotout or tracing should be removed, and the straight lines joining the nails can be woven with any coloured wire, string or thread. This is illustrated on page 27.

Vary satisfactory results occur if thin copper wire is used. The coated wire used for winding motors or transformers is ideal, and can be quite inexpensive if a suitable industrial source of roll ends can be found.

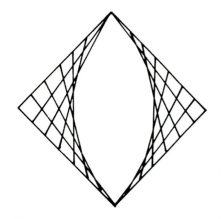

Figure 3.17

4 Interactive computer-aided drafting

4.1 The computer as a drafting device

This chapter introduces ideas for producing programs which will allow you to use the computer as a drafting device. You will use the keyboard as a means of controlling your drawing, but there are a variety of other methods used with commercial drafting packages. These include a **joystick**, **light pen**, **mouse** and **graphics tablet**. There is no room here to discuss how these devices work, but some of the packages which use such devices are discussed in Chapter 5.

Program 4.1 gives a very simple example of a drawing program which allows you to draw shapes using horizontal and vertical lines under the control of the R,L,U and D keys for Right, Left, Up and Down movement respectively.

Program 4.1

```
 10 MODE 4
 20 X=640:Y=512
 30 MOVE X,Y
 40 input$=GET$
 50 IF input$="L" THEN X=X-10
 60 IF input$="R" THEN X=X+10
 70 IF input$="U" THEN Y=Y+10
 80 IF input$="D" THEN Y=Y-10
 90 DRAW X,Y
100 GOTO 40
```

This program introduces the principle of programming the computer keys to draw lines. Line 40 contains the command GET$, which looks for a key being pressed, and lines 50 to 80 increase or decrease the X and Y values by 10, depending on which key has been pressed.

The program has to become much more sophisticated to be of any use. If you add the following lines, pressing E will enable you to erase drawn lines. This is achieved by using the PLOT 7 command in line 170. This command draws a line in the background colour, which effectively erases any line that is drawn over after the E key has been pressed. To end the erasing function you should press the Q key.

```
 85 IF input$="E" THEN GOSUB 120
110 input$=GET$
120 IF input$="L" THEN X=X-10
130 IF input$="R" THEN X=X+10
140 IF input$="U" THEN Y=Y+10
150 IF input$="D" THEN Y=Y-10
160 IF input$="Q" THEN RETURN
170 PLOT 7,X,Y
180 GOTO 120
```

Line 85 introduces the option of pressing E to obtain the erasing routine, which will send the computer to line 120 with the GOSUB command (Go to the SUB-routine found in line 120). The computer then executes the lines 110 to 180 until the Q key is pressed, when it will [RETURN] to the point in the program where the sub-routine was called.

Another way of introducing an erasing routine is to use the GCOL command. The GCOL statement is followed by two numbers separated by a comma. The first number dictates how colour is placed on the screen and the second number decides the colour that appears. A full explanation of the facilities offered by this command is too complex for the purposes of this book, but several of the publications contained in the further reading list on page 69 give more information about this command.

If the following additions are made to the original program (4.1) it produces a simpler erasing facility:

```
85 IF input$="E" THEN GCOL 2,0
95 IF input$="Q" THEN GCOL 0,1
```

Using the cursor keys for control

It is more usual to use the arrow keys (or cursor keys), located at the top right-hand side of the keyboard to control movement on the screen. These keys can be set so that their normal cursor editing function is cancelled and they generate normal ASCII codes. The command *FX4,1 disables the editing function and enables ASCII code generation, when the keys return the following code numbers:

Arrow left   136
Arrow right   137
Arrow down   138
Arrow up   139

To see how these keys can be used to control movement, program 4.1 can be re-written, using the cursor keys as shown in program 4.2.

Program 4.2

```
 10 MODE 4
 15 *FX4,1
 20 X=640:Y=512
 30 MOVE X,Y
 40 input$=GET$
 50 IF input$=CHR$(136) THEN X=X-10
 60 IF input$=CHR$(137) THEN X=X+10
 70 IF input$=CHR$(138) THEN Y=Y-10
 80 IF input$=CHR$(139) THEN Y=Y+10
 90 DRAW X,Y
100 GOTO 40
```

The vertical and horizontal lines are now drawn under the control of the arrow keys. Notice the form that the comparisons in lines 50 to 80 now take. Because we are using the ASCII codes for the keys we have to use the form: compare 'input$' with the CHaracteR whose string is 136, which is written CHR$ (136).

If you interrupt the program and want to use these keys for their normal cursor editing control, you will have to enter the command:

```
*FX4,0 [RETURN]
```

Another useful way of programming the arrow keys is with the use of the INKEY command. This command, followed by a negative number in brackets, will enable you to test to see whether a particular key has been pressed. The *BBC Microcomputer User Guide* gives a list of the negative numbers used to test any particular key. From this list we see that to test for the arrow keys the following numbers are used:

Arrow left   −26
Arrow right −122
Arrow down   −42
Arrow up   −58

Therefore, the command INKEY (−26) would test whether the left-pointing arrow has been pressed.

This form of programming can be tried by re-writing program 4.1 into the form given in program 4.3. Note that the *FX4,1 command is not needed when using the INKEY command.

Program 4.3

```
10 MODE 4
20 X=640:Y=512
30 MOVEX,Y
40 IF INKEY(-26) THEN X=X-1
50 IF INKEY(-122) THEN X=X+1
60 IF INKEY(-42) THEN Y=Y-1
70 IF INKEY(-58) THEN Y=Y+1
80 DRAW X,Y
90 GOTO 40
```

This system is slightly easier to program and is much faster. In fact, you will find it too fast if the increments are kept at 10 as in the previous program, and you will notice that they are reduced to 1 in this version.

This form of programming the cursor keys also has the advantage of allowing two keys to be pressed at once, which will allow lines to be drawn diagonally. Try holding down two arrow keys to give diagonal movement.

A graphics cursor

So far in this section, the only image you get is of the lines you are drawing as they are drawn. Most drafting programs show some form of cursor which can be moved around the screen to locate the positions for drawing lines and other shapes.

We will define a cursor using the user-defined character technique described in Chapter 2 (page 20). At the end of that chapter we defined a 'cross wire' cursor which will be suitable as a graphics cursor. That cursor took the form of the character illustrated in Figure 4.1 and is defined by the command

`VDU 23,224,24,24,60,231,231,60,24,24`

It can be printed on the screen by entering the command VDU 224.

You will remember that the first number following VDU 23 is the code number for the character you are defining, which can be in the range 224 to 255 inclusive.

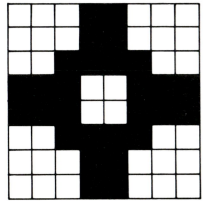

Figure 4.1

Program 4.4 will enable you to move this cursor around the screen under the control of the arrow keys.

Program 4.4

```
 10 MODE4
 20 *FX4,1
 30 VDU23,224,24,24,60,231,231,60,24,24
 40 X=640:Y=512
 50 VDU5:GCOL3,1
 60 REPEAT
 70 MOVEX,Y:PRINT CHR$(224)
 80 input$=GET$
 90 MOVEX,Y:PRINT CHR$(224)
100 IF input$=CHR$(136) THEN X=X-10
110 IF input$=CHR$(137) THEN X=X+10
120 IF input$=CHR$(138) THEN Y=Y-10
130 IF input$=CHR$(139) THEN Y=Y+10
140 UNTIL FALSE
```

This simple program uses the re-defined cursor keys to control the screen movement of the character defined in line 30.

The GCOL3,1 command in line 50 specifies how things are drawn on the screen, and in this program it allows us to draw and then rub out the character (CHR$224) by drawing it in a given position and then re-drawing it in the same position (lines 70 and 90).

The REPEAT–UNTIL FALSE loop, set up in lines 60 and 140, ensures that the program keeps running.

Now that we have a graphics cursor, which can be moved around the screen under the control of the cursor keys, we can make a program that will draw lines with the cursor. The previous examples produced continuous line-drawing, which is not very useful. We will now add to cursor program 4.4 so that we can switch on and switch off a line-drawing procedure.

Make the following additions to program 4.4:

```
140 IF input$="F" THEN PROCfix
150 IF input$="D" THEN PROCdraw
160 UNTIL FALSE
200 DEF PROCfix
210 A=X+16:B=Y-12
220 PLOT 69,A,B
230 ENDPROC
240 DEF PROCdraw
250 MOVE A,B
260 DRAW X+16,Y-12
270 ENDPROC
```

These two PROCEDURES enable you to fix the starting point of a line by pressing the F key to call PROCfix. This will place a point at the start of the line by using the PLOT 69 command in line 220. The co-ordinates A and B are at the centre of the cursor. They are obtained by altering the X and Y co-ordinates which are located at the top left corner of the character defining the graphics cursor. Figure 4.2 illustrates the need for this adjustment to get the line drawn from the centre of the cursor.

The cursor can now be moved to the point where the other end of the line is required and the line drawn by pressing the D key, which

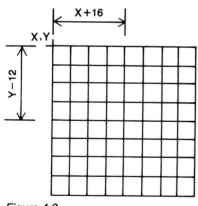

Figure 4.2

calls the PROCEDURE PROCdraw. This MOVEs the computer cursor to point (A,B) and then DRAWs a line to the current position of the graphics cursor, which is given by the current screen co-ordinates of that cursor.

Again, the adjustments (X+16,Y−12) are made to get the line drawn to the centre of the cursor.

Erasing

You will know from experience that a rubber is useful when drawing, and the ability to 'rub out' images made on the VDU would make the program much more useful.

One of the simplest ways of rubbing out is to clear the screen, and this could be done by adding the following lines to the program:

```
160 IF input$="W" THEN PROCwipe
170 UNTIL FALSE
280 DEF PROCwipe
290 CLS
300 ENDPROC
```

This is only useful if the whole screen needs to be wiped clean. We need something which acts more like a rubber, to erase parts of a drawing.

You should now save the program that you have put together so far, on tape or disk, so that we can look at a suitable erasing procedure. Once you have saved the program, type the command NEW[RETURN]. This will clear the memory of the old program so that you can enter a new one.

You should now enter the commands CLS to clear the screen and *FX4,0 to switch the arrow keys back to their cursor editing function. Now enter program 4.5 and run it.

Program 4.5

```
10 MODE4
20 VDU5
30 MOVE450,540:PRINT"RUB ME OUT"
40 VDU23,225,255,129,129,129,129,129,129,255
50 X=20:Y=100
60 REPEAT
70 MOVEX,Y
80 VDU225
90 IF INKEY(-122) THEN X=X+5
100 IF INKEY(-26) THEN X=X-5
110 IF INKEY(-58) THEN Y=Y+5
120 IF INKEY(-42) THEN Y=Y-5
130 VDU 127
140 UNTIL INKEY(-99)
150 END
```

This program places some lettering in the centre of the screen and a small square in the bottom left corner. This square can be moved around using the arrow keys and will rub the lettering out as it passes over it. The 'eraser' square is defined in line 40, and the VDU225 command, in line 80, prints the defined character on the screen. The erasing is done with the VDU 127 command in line 130, which moves the screen cursor back one character and deletes (erases) at that position.

The INKEY(−99) command at line 140 ends the REPEAT−UNTIL loop by looking for a press on the SPACE BAR, which will END the program. It is useful to be able to speed up the movement of the eraser when moving to an area being erased and then slow it down for the actual erasing. This can be done by making the following additions and amendments to the program:

```
 85 INC=1
 86 IF INKEY(-2) THEN INC=5
 90 IF INKEY(-122) THEN X=X+INC
100 IF INKEY(-26) THEN X=X-INC
110 IF INKEY(-58) THEN Y=Y+INC
120 IF INKEY(-42) THEN Y=Y-INC
```

If the program is now run, you will see that pressing the CTRL key while holding down an arrow key will speed up the movement of the 'eraser'. Releasing the CTRL key will slow down the movement for more accurate erasing.

Line 85 sets the increment (INC) to 1, but the INKEY(−2) command in line 86 will increase it to 5 if the CTRL key is pressed.

One other modification is needed to make the 'eraser' of real use. At the moment it erases all the time as it is moved around the screen. This is not very satisfactory, and program 4.6 will allow the erasing facility to be switched on by pressing the 0 key and switched off, or cancelled, with the C key.

Program 4.6

```
 10 MODE4
 20 *FX4,1
 30 VDU 5
 40 MOVE450,540:PRINT"RUB ME OUT"
 50 GCOL3,1
 60 VDU 23,225,255,129,129,129,129,129,129,255
 70 X=20:Y=100
 80 REPEAT
 90 MOVE X,Y:VDU225
100 input$=GET$
110 MOVEX,Y:VDU225
120 IF input$="O" THEN GOSUB 180
130 IF INKEY-122 THEN X=X+10
140 IF INKEY-26 THEN X=X-10
150 IF INKEY-58 THEN Y=Y+10
160 IF INKEY-42 THEN Y=Y-10
170 UNTIL FALSE
180 REPEAT
190 GCOL0,1
200 MOVE X,Y:VDU225
210 input$=GET$
220 IF INKEY-122 THEN X=X+10
230 IF INKEY-26 THEN X=X-10
240 IF INKEY-58 THEN Y=Y+10
250 IF INKEY-42 THEN Y=Y-10
260 VDU127
270 UNTIL input$="C"
280 GCOL3,1
290 RETURN
```

You can now load the drawing program back into the computer, and we will add an erasing PROCEDURE to it. The version given here will be the simplest one, but you can develop some of the other ideas presented to make it more useful.

The drawing facilities developed so far are now given in program 4.7, but if you have saved program 4.4 with the additions and amendments, as suggested earlier, you need only add the new lines which call and define the erasing PROCEDURE.

Lines 315 and 415 have been added to stop the X and Y values within PROCerase affecting the value of X and Y in the main program. The LOCAL command in line 315 tells the computer that X and Y must be restored to the value they had before entering the PROCEDURE, and the *FX21,0 command clears the keyboard buffer. If this is not done, the cursor moves around by itself for a little while when returning to the main program. If you would like to see the effect of this command, run the program without line 415.

Program 4.7

```
 10 MODE4
 20 *FX4,1
 30 VDU23,224,24,24,60,231,231,60,24,24
 40 X=640:Y=512
 50 VDU5:GCOL3,1
 60 REPEAT
 70 MOVEX,Y:PRINT CHR$(224)
 80 input$=GET$
 90 MOVEX,Y:PRINT CHR$(224)
100 IF input$=CHR$(136) THEN X=X-10
110 IF input$=CHR$(137) THEN X=X+10
120 IF input$=CHR$(138) THEN Y=Y-10
130 IF input$=CHR$(139) THEN Y=Y+10
140 IF input$="F" THEN PROCfix
150 IF input$="D" THEN PROCdraw
160 IF input$="W" THEN PROCwipe
165 IF input$="E" THEN PROCerase
170 UNTIL FALSE
200 DEF PROCfix
210 A=X+16:B=Y-12
220 PLOT69,A,B
230 ENDPROC
240 DEF PROCdraw
250 MOVEA,B
260 DRAW X+16,Y-12
270 ENDPROC
280 DEF PROCwipe
290 CLS
300 ENDPROC
310 DEF PROCerase
315 LOCALX,Y
320 VDU23,225,255,129,129,129,129,129,129,255
330 X=20:Y=100
340 REPEAT
350 MOVE X,Y
360 VDU 225
370 IF INKEY(-122) THEN X=X+5
380 IF INKEY(-26) THEN X=X-5
390 IF INKEY(-58) THEN Y=Y+5
400 IF INKEY(-42) THEN Y=Y-5
410 VDU 127
415 *FX21,0
420 UNTIL INKEY(-99)
430 ENDPROC
```

The following is a summary of the control keys for program 4.7:

CURSOR KEYS control the movement of the graphics cursor and the eraser.

F	fixes one end of a line.
D	draws the line.
W	wipes the whole screen
E	calls the erasing procedure.
SPACE BAR	cancels the erasing procedure.

PROCEDURES for drawing circles

You can see how a program can be built up gradually by adding PROCEDURES to offer more facilities. At the moment it is limited to drawing straight lines, so we will add a circle-drawing PROCEDURE which will make the program more useful.

Make the following additions to program 4.7. You should be able to understand what is happening, but you can still use the program even if you do not fully understand how it works.

```
155 IF input$="C" THEN PROCcircle
440 DEF PROCcircle
450 MOVE X,Y:PRINTCHR$(224)
460 P=X+16:Q=Y-12:R=0
470 PLOT 69,P,Q
480 VDU 29,P;Q;
490 input$=GET$
500 IF input$=CHR$(137) PLOT 69,R,0:R=R+10:
        PLOT 69,R,0
510 IF input$=CHR$(136) PLOT 69,R,0:R=R-10:
        PLOT 69,R,0
520 IF input$=CHR$(138) PLOT 69,0,R:R=R-10:
        PLOT 69,0,R
530 IF input$=CHR$(139) PLOT 69,0,R:R=R+10:
        PLOT 69,0,R
540 IF input$="D" THEN PROCdrawcircle
550 GOTO 490
560 DEF PROCdrawcircle
570 MOVE R,0
580 GCOL 0,1
590 FOR angle%=0 TO 360 STEP 10
600 angle=RAD(angle%)
610 DRAW R*COS(angle),R*SIN(angle)
620 NEXT
630 VDU 29,0;0;
640 GCOL 3,1
650 MOVE X,Y:PRINTCHR$(224)
660 GOTO 170
670 ENDPROC
```

The circle-drawing PROCEDURE is called by pressing the C key. The centre of the circle is at the current position of the cursor. A point can be taken out in any one of four directions using the arrow keys. This point controls the radius of the circle, and once it is in position pressing the D key will cause a circle to be drawn. The program then returns to the original cursor moving under the control of the arrow keys.

Exercises

1 Use the amended program 4.7 to produce a variety of drawings. If you have a suitable screen dump ROM and a dot matrix printer, add a printer dump routine so that you can print the screen image.
2 Modify the program to use the better erasing facilities discussed.
3 Add instructions which will come up on the screen to help remind

the user of the keys that have to be pressed to operate the program. This can be done by having an instruction page or by setting up a text window for the instructions. A suitable window would be set by using the command

```
VDU 28,0,31,39,28
```

Text will be printed in this window and can be erased with the CLS command, without affecting the graphics on the screen. More details about setting up text windows can be found in the *BBC Microcomputer User Guide*.

Drawing ellipses and arcs

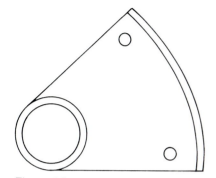

Figure 4.3

The drafting program is now becoming a useful facility; and you could make it even more versatile by adding other features. The inclusion of ellipse and circular arc drawings might be worthwhile additions so that drawings of the type shown in Figure 4.3 can be produced. A simple arc drawing PROCEDURE can be added to the main drafting program by adding the following lines:

```
25  VDU 28,0,31,40,30
545 IF input$="A" THEN PROCarc
680 DEFPROCarc
690 VDU 4
700 INPUT"ANGLE AT START OF ARC",AS
710 INPUT"ANGLE AT END OF ARC",AE
720 A1=RAD(AS)
730 IF R<1 THEN R=-(R)
740 MOVE R*COS(A1),R*SIN(A1)
750 GCOL 0,1
760 FOR angle%=AS TO AE STEP 10
770 angle=RAD(angle%)
780 DRAW R*COS(angle),R*SIN(angle)
790 NEXT
800 CLS:VDU 5
810 VDU 29,0,0;
820 GCOL 3,1
830 MOVE X,Y:PRINT CHR$(224)
840 GOTO 170
850 ENDPROC
```

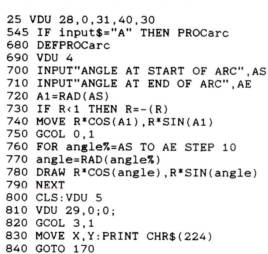

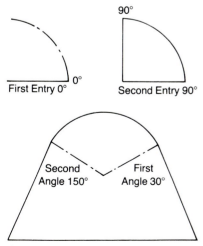

Figure 4.4

The PROCEDURE, PROCarc, is called from within PROCcircle by adding line 545. To begin with, once the main cursor is located at the centre for the arc, key C is pressed to call PROCcircle, and the radius of the arc can be set using the moving point, as for drawing a circle. When this is set the A key is pressed and a prompt, asking for the angle at the start of the arc, appears at the bottom of the screen. Figure 4.4 indicates the angle to be entered.

The number is entered, followed by [RETURN], and a second prompt requests the angle at the end of the arc. This angle is again entered, followed by [RETURN]. The arc is now drawn and the program returns to the main cursor under the control of the arrow keys.

One or two of the additional program lines might need explanation:
- 25 Sets up a text window at the bottom of the screen in which the prompts appear.
- 690 VDU4 frees the text cursor so that it will print letters in the text window.

730 Converts negative values for R to positive, for use in the calculations in lines 740 and 780.
800 Clears text from the text window and rejoins the graphics and text cursors with the VDU 5 command.
810 Resets the graphics origin to its normal position.

Cursor co-ordinates and lettering

Two more simple additions to the program are worth mentioning before ending the development of this drafting program. For accurate location of the cursor a display of the X and Y co-ordinates would be useful. This would help to produce correct alignment and sizing on drawings. The ability to add lettering to a drawing is another very useful facility and can easily be added to our program.

The following lines should be added to the main program to extend it to include the two facilities mentioned above:

```
 65 PROCprintxy
185 IF input$="L" THEN PROClettering
860 DEF PROCprintxy
870 VDU 4
875 VDU23;10,32,0;0;0;
880 PRINT TAB(1,1) X,Y
890 VDU 5
900 ENDPROC
910 DEF PROClettering
920 MOVE X,Y
930 REPEAT
940 L$=GET$:PRINT L$;
945 REM REPEAT UNTIL COPY KEY IS PRESSED
950 UNTIL INKEY(-106)
960 X=640:Y=512
970 ENDPROC
```

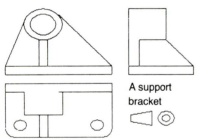

A support bracket

Figure 4.5

Hidden detail lines

You might think of other PROCEDURES you would like to add to extend the range of facilities. The most obvious is the inclusion of one to produce hidden detail lines. You have used the PLOT 21 command to produce a dotted line in section 2.

You might like to add the option of obtaining a print out of any drawings made on the screen on a dot matrix printer. This could be done using a suitable screen dump ROM as discussed in Chapter 3. Figures 4.5 to 4.7 show some examples of drawings produced with this program which have been printed out on a dot matrix printer.

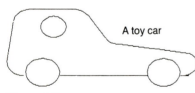

A toy car

Figure 4.6

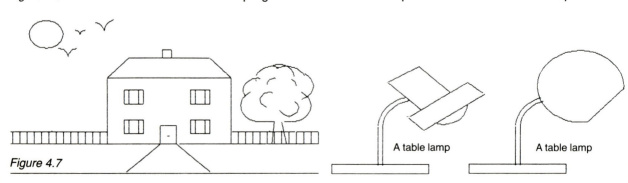

A table lamp

A table lamp

Figure 4.7

4.2 Rubber banding

This is the name given to a technique used in many drafting programs where one end of a line is fixed and the other end can be moved around and fixed under the control of the computer keyboard. It is similar to the basic drawing PROCEDURE given in program 4.7, but it uses a movable line, rather than a line drawn between two previously fixed points. Program 4.8 demonstrates this technique.

Program 4.8
```
 10 MODE0
 20 *FX4,1
 30 VDU28,0,31,39,30
 40 INPUT"START POINT"XS,YS
 50 CLS
 60 X=640:Y=512
 70 GCOL 3,1
 80 MOVEXS,YS:DRAW X,Y
 90 REPEAT
100 input$=GET$
110 MOVEXS,YS:DRAW X,Y
120 IF input$="R" THEN GOTO 40
130 IF INKEY(-26) THEN X=X-5
140 IF INKEY(-122) THEN X=X+5
150 IF INKEY(-42) THEN Y=Y-5
160 IF INKEY(-58) THEN Y=Y+5
170 MOVEXS,YS:DRAW X,Y
180 UNTIL INKEY(-99)
190 GCOL 0,1
200 MOVE XS,YS:DRAW X,Y
210 GCOL 3,1
220 XS=X:YS=Y
230 GOTO 80
```

This program has been kept very simple so that it demonstrates the principle of rubber banding. Initially you will be asked for the co-ordinates of the starting point for the line. These can be entered in one of two ways: 200,350 [RETURN] or 200 [RETURN] 350 [RETURN].

A line will now be drawn between these co-ordinates and the centre of the screen, which are a pair of co-ordinates set in line 60. It is these co-ordinates which can now be altered by pressing the arrow keys, so moving the 'free' end of the line. When this end of the line is in the required position pressing the space bar will draw the line. The 'free' end of the line now becomes the fixed end of a new line. This is accomplished in line 220 where XS and YS are set to equal X and Y, respectively. If you press R, the end of a new line can be located in a different position by inputting new co-ordinates.

The program could now be developed to include other facilities such as erasing, circle drawing and a current X,Y co-ordinate read-out. You will notice that the flashing cursor is visible throughout the program, and one initial improvement would be to add a command to switch the cursor off. You have used a command for this in previous programs (pages 12 and 30) and you can refer back if you have forgotten it.

4.3 Pick and drag

This is another very useful technique used in **interactive drafting** programs. As the name implies, small drawings, representing objects,

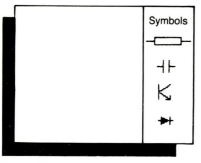

Figure 4.8

can be selected or picked and dragged across the screen to be fixed in a chosen position. One typical use for this technique is in producing electronic circuit diagrams where the electronic components can be displayed in an area on the screen. Appropriate components are then picked and dragged into position on the screen. Figure 4.8 shows a typical screen layout for such a program.

One of the best ways of producing the small symbols for the components is to use the PLOT command. There are many options available within the PLOT command, and we have already used some of them in previous programs. The PLOT command is described in the *BBC Microcomputer User Guide*.

The following short program illustrates how the PLOT command can be used to produce a resistor symbol. The PLOT command takes the following form: PLOT n,X,Y, where n dictates which option is chosen and X and Y specify the point where the symbol is to be plotted. Initially we will use the following PLOT options.

PLOT 0 move relative to the last point.
PLOT 1 draw a line relative to the last point.

Therefore, PLOT 0,200,300 would move the cursor to the point given by co-ordinates 200,300, and PLOT 1,500,700 would draw from the co-ordinates 200,300 to 500,700.

Enter each of these commands, in sequence, into the computer to see this happening.

A resistor symbol could be defined using the following plot statements:

PLOT 1,16,0
PLOT 1,0,12
PLOT 1,72,0
PLOT 1,0,−24
PLOT 1,−72,0
PLOT 1,0,12
PLOT 0,72,0
PLOT 1,16,0

Figure 4.9 shows how this sequence of PLOT statements builds up the resistor symbol.

Program 4.9 places the resistor symbol on the screen.

Program 4.9

```
10 MODE0
20 MOVE 500,600
30 PLOT1,16,0:PLOT1,0,12:PLOT1,72,0:PLOT1,0,-24:
       PLOT1,-72,0:PLOT1,0,12
40 PLOT0,72,0:PLOT1,16,0
```

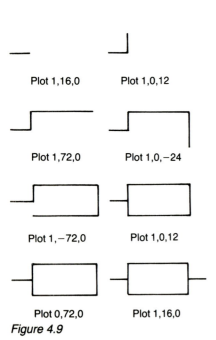

Figure 4.9

We now need a method of moving the symbol around the screen, under the control of the keyboard, and then the option to fix the symbol in a given position. Program 4.10 shows how this can be done. The arrow keys move the resistor symbol around the screen, and pressing F will fix the symbol in the current position.

Program 4.10

```
 10 MODE0
 20 *FX4,1
 30 VDU5
 40 X=50:Y=50
 50 GCOL3,1
 60 PROCresistor(X,Y)
 70 REPEAT
 80 input$=GET$
 90 PROCinput
100 UNTIL input$="Q"
110 MODE7:END
120 DEF PROCinput
130 IF input$="F" THEN PROCfix ELSE
         PROCresistor(X,Y)
140 IF INKEY(-26) THEN X=X-5
150 IF INKEY(-122) THEN X=X+5
160 IF INKEY(-58) THEN Y=Y+5
170 IF INKEY(-42) THEN Y=Y-5
180 PROCresistor(X,Y)
190 ENDPROC
200 DEF PROCfix
210 GCOL 0,1:PROCresistor(X,Y)
220 GCOL 3,1
230 X=50:Y=50
240 ENDPROC
250 DEF PROCresistor(X,Y)
260 MOVEX,Y
270 PLOT1,16,0:PLOT1,0,12:PLOT1,72,0:PLOT1,0,-24
280 PLOT 1,-72,0:PLOT1,0,12:PLOT0,72,0:PLOT1,16,0
290 ENDPROC
```

For a circuit-drafting program we need to be able to select a number of components, and program 4.11 demonstrates how this could be developed.

Program 4.11

```
 10 MODE0
 20 *FX4,1
 30 VDU28,0,31,79,30
 40 PROCsymbol(1,50,400)
 50 PROCsymbol(2,80,500)
 60 PROCchoosesymbol
 70 X=50:Y=50
 80 GCOL3,1
 90 PROCsymbol(S,X,Y)
100 REPEAT
110 input$=GET$
120 PROCinput
130 UNTIL input$="Q"
140 MODE7:END
150 DEF PROCinput
160 IF input$="F" THEN PROCfix ELSE PROCsymbol(S,X,Y)
170 IF INKEY(-26) THEN X=X-5
180 IF INKEY(-122) THEN X=X+5
190 IF INKEY(-58) THEN Y=Y+5
200 IF INKEY(-42) THEN Y=Y-5
210 PROCsymbol(S,X,Y)
220 ENDPROC
230 DEF PROCfix
240 GCOL 0,1:PROCsymbol(S,X,Y)
250 GCOL 3,1
```

```
260 X=50:Y=50
270 GOTO60
280 ENDPROC
290 DEF PROCsymbol(S,X,Y)
300 MOVE X,Y
310 ON S GOSUB 340,370
320 ENDPROC
330 MOVEX,Y
340 PLOT1,16,0:PLOT1,0,12:PLOT1,72,0:PLOT1,0,-24
350 PLOT 1,-72,0:PLOT1,0,12:PLOT0,72,0:PLOT1,16,0
360 RETURN
370 PLOT1,16,0:PLOT0,0,20:PLOT1,0,-40:PLOT0,16,40
380 PLOT1,0,-40:PLOT0,0,20:PLOT1,16,0
390 RETURN
400 DEF PROCchoosesymbol
410 PRINT"WHICH COMPONENT? Resistor(R); Capacitor(C)"
420 input$=GET$
430 IF input$="R" THEN S=1
440 IF input$="C" THEN S=2
450 CLS
460 ENDPROC
```

This program is still lacking in symbol options and a method of drawing lines to link them. We would also need to have the symbols available in both the vertical and horizontal orientations.

Exercises

1 Develop program 4.11 so that you can place the resistor and capacitor symbol in both the horizontal and vertical positions, and add a method of drawing lines to link them. You could also add the facility to select symbols for a battery and a transistor, so that you can draw circuits like the ones shown in Figure 4.10.

2 The program can be used for other forms of drafting such as room layout plans. Re-write the program so that you have suitable symbols for laying out the plan of a kitchen or a workshop.

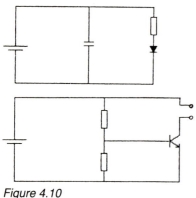

Figure 4.10

4.4 An electronic circuit-drafting program

The ideas presented in program 4.11 are more fully developed in program 4.12, which is a very useful circuit-drafting facility. It is quite a long program but is well worth entering into the computer. Care should be taken to ensure that it is entered without errors, as the smallest typing mistake, such as a missing comma or a comma instead of a semi-colon, will result in the program failing to run. Once the program has been entered and run it should be saved on tape or disk.

The program is extensive and offers some facilities which have not been discussed previously in this book. Some of these use advanced programming, but the procedures can be taken as self-contained units and used in other programs which you may structure.

Figure 4.11 shows examples produced with program 4.12 which were printed out on an Epson FX-80 printer. The quality is acceptable and the diagrams were produced more quickly than if they had been drawn by hand. There is also the advantage that the diagrams can be saved on tape or disk and loaded back in at a later date for re-printing or modification before reprinting.

Before loading this program, enter into the computer:

PAGE=&1500 [RETURN]

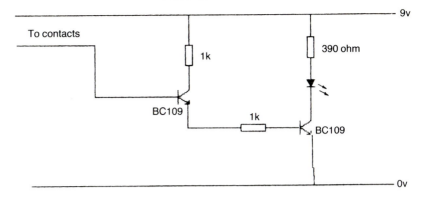

Figure 4.11 Circuit diagrams produced with program 4.12

This will ensure that there is enough memory space for the program if the computer has a **disk interface**.

The arrow keys control the movement of the cursor around the screen, and the options listed at the bottom of the screen are selected by pressing the first letter of their names. Lines can be drawn using the four keys adjacent to the arrow keys: '\' draws up, '_' to the right, '[' to the left and ']' down. Figure 14.12 shows the position of these keys on the keyboard.

Line erasing can be obtained if the SHIFT key is held down with any of these keys.

The screen dump is obtained by pressing P, and the command in line 790 of the program is for the Computer Concepts Printmaster ROM. This command will have to be changed if another method of dumping the screen is used.

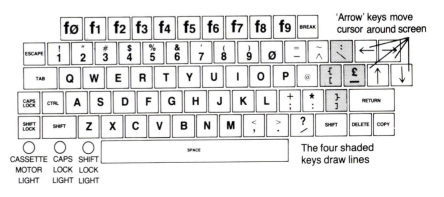

Figure 4.12 The position of the arrow keys on the BBC keyboard

51

Program 4.12

```
  10 MODE0
  20 DIM COD 30
  30 VDU28,0,31,79,29:REM SET UP TEXT WINDOW
  40 VDU24,0;32;1279;1023;
  50 CLS
  60 VDU23,135,0,0,0,0,0,0,0,0
  70 *DIR C
  80 *FX4,1
  90 MOVE 600,500:FLAG=0
 100 PROCMENU
 110 ON ERROR GOTO 1450
 120 REPEAT
 130 PROCCURSOR
 140 KEY=GET
 150 PROCCURSOR
 160 IF KEY=&88 THEN PLOT0,-4,0:GOTO460
 170 IF KEY =&89 THEN PLOT0,4,0:GOTO460
 180 IF KEY=&8B THEN PLOT0,0,4:GOTO460
 190 IF KEY=&8A THEN PLOT0,0,-4:GOTO460
 200 IF KEY=&5B THEN PLOT1,-4,0:GOTO460
 210 IF KEY =&5F THEN PLOT1,4,0:GOTO460
 220 IF KEY=&5C THEN PLOT1,0,4:GOTO460
 230 IF KEY=&5D THEN PLOT1,0,-4:GOTO460
 240 IF KEY=&7B THEN PLOT3,-4,0:GOTO460
 250 IF KEY=&60 THEN PLOT3,4,0:GOTO460
 260 IF KEY=&7C THEN PLOT3,0,4:GOTO460
 270 IF KEY=&7D THEN PLOT3,0,-4:GOTO460
 280 IF KEY=&0D THEN PROCMENU:GOTO460
 290 IF KEY=&72 OR KEY=&52 THEN CLS:PRINT"RESISTOR:":PROCDIRECTION:
     PROCRESISTOR(DIR):PROCMENU:GOTO460
 300 IF KEY=&63 OR KEY=&43 THEN CLS:PRINT"CAPACITOR:":PROCDIRECTION:
     PROCCAPACITOR(DIR):PROCMENU:GOTO460
 310 IF(KEY=&74 OR KEY=&54) AND FLAG=0 THEN CLS:PRINT"TRANSISTOR:
     MOVE THE CURSOR TO THE LOCATION OF THE 'BASE' TERMINAL AND PRESS
     'T' AGAIN":LET FLAG=1:GOTO460
 320 IF (KEY=&74 OR KEY=&54) AND FLAG=1 THEN CLS:PROCTRANSISTOR:
     LET FLAG=0:PROCMENU:GOTO460
 330 IF (KEY=&4B OR KEY=&6B) AND FLAG=0 THEN CLS:PRINT
     "CONFIRM WIPE WHOLE DISPLAY BY PRESSING'K' AGAIN":FLAG=2:GOTO 460
 340 IF (KEY=&4B OR KEY=&6B)AND FLAG=2 THEN CLG:PROCMENU:GOTO460
 350 IF KEY=&57 OR KEY=&77 THEN PRINT"WRITING TEXT AT CURRENT CURSOR
     POSITION...";'"PRESS <COPY> TO END TEXT":PROCTEXT:PROCMENU:GOTO460
 360 IF KEY=&64 OR KEY=&44 THEN PRINT"DIODE...":PROCDIRECTION:
     PROCDIODE(DIR):PROCMENU:GOTO460
 370 IF KEY=&42 OR KEY=&62 THEN PRINT"THE BATTERY WILL APPEAR WITH THE
     NEGATIVE TERMINAL AT THE CURSOR...":PROCDIRECTION:PROCBATTERY(DIR):
     PROCMENU:GOTO460
 380 IF KEY=&50 OR KEY=&70 THEN CLS:PROCPRINT:PROCMENU:MOVE600,500:
     PROCCURSOR:PROCCURSOR:GOTO460
 390 IF KEY=&53 OR KEY=&73 THEN PROCSAVE:PROCMENU:GOTO460
 400 IF KEY=&6C OR KEY=&4C THEN PROCLOAD:PROCMENU:GOTO460
 410 IF(KEY=&45 OR KEY=&65) AND FLAG=0 THEN PRINT"CURRENT CURSOR
     POSITION IS BOTTOM LEFT CORNER OF AREA TO BE ERASED":
     POSX1=?&310+256*?&311:POSY1=?&312+?&313*256:PRINT"MOVE CURSOR TO TOP
     RIGHT OF AREA AND PRESS 'E' AGAIN":FLAG=3:GOTO460
 420 IF (KEY=&45 OR KEY=&65) AND FLAG=3 THEN PROCERASE:PROCMENU:GOTO460
 430 IF KEY=&41 OR KEY=&61 THEN PRINT"ARROW: The current cursor position
     is the tip of the arrow...":PROCDIRECTION:PROCARROW(DIR):PROCMENU:
     GOTO460
 440 IF(KEY=&4F OR KEY=&6F) AND FLAG=0 THEN PRINT"OPERATIONAL AMPLIFIER";
     '"PLACE CURSOR MIDWAY BETWEEN POSITIVE AND NEGATIVE INPUTS, THEN
     PRESS 'O' AGAIN":FLAG=4:GOTO460
 450 IF (KEY=&4F OR KEY=&6F) AND FLAG=4 THEN PROCAMP:PROCMENU:GOTO460
 460 UNTIL FALSE
 470 DEFPROCMENU
```

```
 480 FLAG=0
 490 CLS:PRINT"Resistor..Capacitor..Write text..Transistor..Arrow..Diode
     ..Battery..OP-amp.........Clear screen(K)..Save/Load to tape/disc
     ..Print screen..Erase area...":ENDPROC
 500 DEFPROCCURSOR
 510 PLOT0,-16,-16
 520 PLOT2,32,32
 530 PLOT0,-32,0
 540 PLOT2,32,-32
 550 PLOT0,-16,16
 560 ENDPROC
 570 DEFPROCDIRECTION
 580 PRINT"Up, Down, Left or Right?"
 590 A$=GET$
 600 IF A$="R" OR A$="r" THEN DIR=1:ENDPROC
 610 IF A$="L" OR A$="l" THEN DIR=2:ENDPROC
 620 IF A$="D" OR A$="d" THEN DIR=3:ENDPROC
 630 IF A$="U" OR A$="u" THEN DIR=4:ENDPROC
 640 GOTO 580
 650 DEFPROCDIODE(X)
 660 ON X GOSUB 680,690,700,710
 670 ENDPROC
 680 PLOT1,8,0:PLOT0,0,12:PLOT1,0,-24:PLOT81,24,12:PLOT0,0,12:
     PLOT1,0,-24:PLOT0,0,12:PLOT1,8,0:RETURN
 690 PLOT1,-8,0:PLOT0,0,12:PLOT1,0,-24:PLOT81,-24,12:PLOT0,0,12:
     PLOT1,0,-24:PLOT0,0,12:PLOT1,-8,0:RETURN
 700 PLOT1,0,-8:PLOT0,12,0:PLOT1,-24,0:PLOT81,12,-24:PLOT0,12,0:
     PLOT1,-24,0:PLOT0,12,0:PLOT1,0,-8:RETURN
 710 PLOT1,0,8:PLOT0,12,0:PLOT1,-24,0:PLOT81,12,24:PLOT0,12,0:
     PLOT1,-24,0:PLOT0,12,0:PLOT1,0,8:RETURN
 720 DEFPROCBATTERY(X)
 730 ON X GOSUB 750,760,770,780
 740 ENDPROC
 750 PLOT1,8,0:PLOT0,0,-12:PLOT1,0,24:PLOT0,16,12:PLOT1,0,-48:
     PLOT0,0,24:PLOT1,8,0:RETURN
 760 PLOT1,-8,0:PLOT0,0,-12:PLOT1,0,24:PLOT0,-16,12:PLOT1,0,-48:
     PLOT0,0,24:PLOT1,-8,0:RETURN
 770 PLOT1,0,-8:PLOT0,12,0:PLOT1,-24,0:PLOT0,-12,-16:PLOT1,48,0:
     PLOT0,-24,0:PLOT1,0,-8:RETURN
 780 PLOT1,0,8:PLOT0,12,0:PLOT1,-24,0:PLOT0,-12,16:PLOT1,48,0:
     PLOT0,-24,0:PLOT1,0,8:RETURN
 790 DEFPROCPRINT
 800 *GDUMP0 0 1 1 20
 810 ENDPROC
 820 DEFPROCSAVE
 830 CLS:INPUT"ENTER FILENAME";B$
 840 IF B$="" THEN ENDPROC
 850 $COD="SAVE "+B$+" 3000 7FFF"
 860 X%=COD MOD 256:Y%=COD DIV 256
 870 CALL &FFF7
 880 ENDPROC
 890 DEFPROCLOAD
 900 CLS:INPUT"ENTER FILENAME";B$
 910 IF B$="" THEN ENDPROC
 920 $COD="LOAD "+B$
 930 X%=COD MOD 256:Y%=COD DIV 256
 940 CALL &FFF7:ENDPROC
 950 DEFPROCCAPACITOR(DIR)
 960 ON DIR GOSUB 980,1000,1010,1030
 970 ENDPROC
 980 PLOT1,16,0:PLOT0,0,20:PLOT1,0,-40:PLOT0,16,40:PLOT1,0,-40:
     PLOT0,0,20:PLOT1,16,0
 990 RETURN
1000 PLOT0,-48,0:GOSUB980:PLOT0,-48,0:RETURN
1010 PLOT1,0,-16:PLOT0,16,0:PLOT1,-32,0:PLOT0,32,-16:PLOT1,-32,0:
     PLOT0,16,0:PLOT1,0,-16
```

```
1020 RETURN
1030 PLOT0,0,48:GOSUB1010:PLOT0,0,48:RETURN
1040 RETURN
1050 DEFPROCTRANSISTOR
1060 PRINT"Npn or Pnp?":TYPE$=GET$:IF TYPE$<>"N" AND TYPE$<>"P"
     THEN GOTO 1060
1070 PRINT"Left or Right?":DIR$=GET$:IF DIR$<>"L" AND DIR$<>"R"
     THEN GOTO 1070
1080 IF TYPE$="N" AND DIR$="L" THEN PROCTRA:ENDPROC
1090 IF TYPE$="N" AND DIR$="R" THEN PROCTRB:ENDPROC
1100 IF TYPE$="P" AND DIR$="L" THEN PROCTRC:ENDPROC
1110 IF TYPE$="P" AND DIR$="R" THEN PROCTRD:ENDPROC
1120 ENDPROC
1130 DEFPROCTRA
1140 PLOT0,0,-24:PLOT1,0,48:PLOT0,-32,0:PLOT1,32,-24:PLOT1,-32,-24:
     PLOT0,12,0:PLOT1,-12,0:PLOT1,0,12:PLOT0,0,-12:ENDPROC
1150 DEFPROCTRB
1160 PLOT0,0,-24:PLOT1,0,48:PLOT0,32,0:PLOT1,-32,-24:PLOT1,32,-24:
     PLOT0,-12,0:PLOT1,12,0:PLOT1,0,12:PLOT0,0,-12:ENDPROC
1170 DEFPROCTRC
1180 PLOT0,0,24:PLOT1,0,-48:PLOT0,-32,0:PLOT1,32,24:PLOT1,-32,24:
     PLOT0,24,-8:PLOT1,0,-12:PLOT1,-12,0:PLOT0,-12,20:ENDPROC
1190 DEFPROCTRD
1200 PLOT0,0,24:PLOT1,0,-48:PLOT0,32,0:PLOT1,-32,24:PLOT1,32,24:
     PLOT0,-24,-8:PLOT1,0,-12:PLOT1,12,0:PLOT0,12,20:ENDPROC
1210 DEFPROCTEXT
1220 VDU5
1230 REPEAT
1240 A$=GET$:PRINTA$;:UNTIL ASC(A$)=&87:VDU4:ENDPROC
1250 DEFPROCERASE
1260 POSX2=?&310+?&311*256:POSY2=?&312+?&313*256
1270 PLOT4,POSX1,POSY1:PLOT4,POSX1,POSY2:PLOT87,POSX2,POSY2:
     PLOT4,POSX2,POSY1:PLOT87,POSX1,POSY1
1280 ENDPROC
1290 DEFPROCARROW(X)
1300 ON X GOSUB 1320,1330,1340,1350
1310 ENDPROC
1320 PLOT1,-32,0:PLOT0,24,8:PLOT1,8,-8:PLOT1,-8,-8:RETURN
1330 PLOT1,32,0:PLOT0,-24,8:PLOT1,-8,-8:PLOT1,8,-8:RETURN
1340 PLOT1,0,32:PLOT0,8,-24:PLOT1,-8,-8:PLOT1,-8,8:RETURN
1350 PLOT1,0,-32:PLOT0,8,24:PLOT1,-8,8:PLOT1,-8,-8:RETURN
1360 DEFPROCAMP
1370 PLOT0,0,48:PLOT1,0,-96
1380 PRINT"LEFT OR RIGHT?":A=GET:IF A=&4C OR A=&6C THEN GOSUB
     1400 ELSE GOSUB 1410
1390 ENDPROC
1400 PLOT1,-96,48:PLOT1,96,48:PLOT0,-96,-48:RETURN
1410 PLOT1,96,48:PLOT1,-96,48:PLOT0,96,-48:RETURN
1420 PLOT0,0,48:PLOT1,0,-96
1430 *DIR C
1440 PROCCURSOR:GOTO100
1450 PRINT"IF YOU WANT TO RE-ENTER THE PROGRAM WITHOUT CLEARING
     THE SCREEN,TYPE 'GOTO1430'";
1460 *DIR$
1470 STOP
1480 DEFPROCRESISTOR(X)
1490 ON X GOSUB 1510,1520,1530,1540
1500 ENDPROC
1510 PLOT1,8,0:PLOT1,0,12:PLOT1,72,0:PLOT1,0,-24:PLOT1,-72,0:
     PLOT1,0,12:PLOT0,72,0:PLOT1,8,0:RETURN
1520 PLOT0,-88,0:GOSUB1510:PLOT0,-88,0:RETURN
1530 PLOT1,0,-8:PLOT1,10,0:PLOT1,0,-72:PLOT1,-20,0:PLOT1,0,72:
     PLOT1,10,0:PLOT0,0,-72:PLOT1,0,-8:RETURN
1540 PLOT0,0,88:GOSUB1530:PLOT0,0,88:RETURN
```

From D. Smith, BBC Basic for Beginners, *1983.*

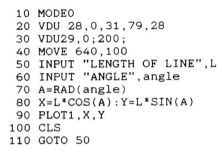

4.5 Isometric drawing

An isometric drawing is a three-dimensional representation of an object which is usually produced using a T-square and a 30 degree set square. Figure 4.13 shows an isometric drawing of a simple bracket.

Program 4.13

```
10 MODE0
20 VDU 28,0,31,79,28
30 VDU29,0;200;
40 MOVE 640,100
50 INPUT "LENGTH OF LINE",L
60 INPUT "ANGLE",angle
70 A=RAD(angle)
80 X=L*COS(A):Y=L*SIN(A)
90 PLOT1,X,Y
100 CLS
110 GOTO 50
```

Figure 4.13

Program 4.13 can be used to produce simple isometric drawings. The program works by drawing lines from given lengths and angles.

When running the program you will first be asked to enter the length of the line. Once this has been entered you will be asked for the angle. This angle will vary depending on the current position of the graphics cursor and where you wish the line being drawn to end. When producing simple rectangular isometric drawings the angle entered (in degrees) will be one of the following: 30,90,150,210,270,330. Figure 4.14 shows how these angles are derived.

If the following lengths and angles are entered into the program in the sequence given, a rectangular block will be drawn in isometric projection. You will notice that the last but one entry does not produce a line. It draws over one of the lines to get into position for drawing the last line. This demonstrates one of the many weaknesses of the program as it stands.

Figure 4.14

Length	Angle	Length	Angle
300	30	200	90
200	90	300	30
300	210	200	330
200	270	300	210
200	150	200	150

Figure 4.15 shows some drawings produced with this simple program.

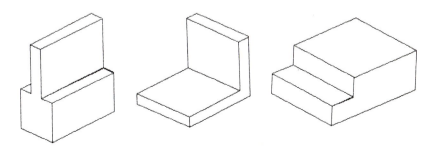

Figure 4.15

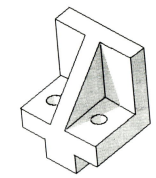

Figure 4.16

Exercises
1. Use program 4.13 to produce a variety of isometric drawings. Can you modify it so that the starting position can be input by you, rather than being fixed, as it is at the moment, by line 40?
2. Program 4.13, as it stands, is a very elementary one and needs to be extended to make it of any real use. Build the program up so that it will make the production of isometric drawings easier and enable you to produce more complex shapes. You will need to structure a control section and make the line-drawing facility, given in the program, a procedure which is called when a particular key is pressed. Some of the procedures used in the previous drafting program (4.7) could also be added here to give a movable cursor and an erasing facility. You might also like to add an ellipse-drawing procedure, so that drawings like the one shown in Figure 4.16 can be produced.

Three-dimensional graphics

Program 4.13 can be used to produce three-dimensional drawings, but it is of little use other than for producing simple 'computer sketches'. Programs to produce true three-dimensional computer graphics are much more complex and involve quite difficult mathematical formulae. The BBC micro-computer lacks the memory space and processing speed to produce anything but the most basic of wire-frame images, but the fundamental principles can be demonstrated.

True three-dimensional computer graphics allow the user to manipulate the screen image so that it can be scaled, rotated and viewed from any angle and also allow the shape to be modified. This form of computer graphics manipulation is very demanding of memory space because the information needed to draw the object has to be held as a vast data bank of numbers.

The computer is also required to perform many complex calculations at high speed to rotate the resulting three-dimensional image, which is then plotted from the data. The amount of memory and processing power required increases in proportion to the complexity and realism of the image. If colour is required, then only the most powerful computers are capable of producing and manipulating advanced three-dimensional graphic images.

Three-dimensional drawing requires the use of three axes. We have already used two for some of our drawings – the X and Y axes to give co-ordinates for length across the screen and height up the screen. A three-dimensional drawing, however, also requires depth, and these co-ordinates are given along a Z axis, as shown in Figure 4.17.

A simple cube of 400 screen units side length would have co-ordinates as shown in the table on page 57. Note that the origin for the three axes is usually located at the centre of the three-dimensional object, and the Z axis co-ordinates are positive going away from the viewer and, therefore, negative coming towards the viewer.

Program 4.14 allows you to rotate a three-dimensional wire-frame image of a cube by pressing any key.

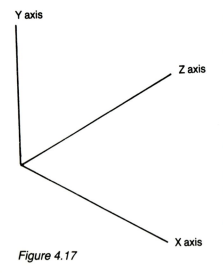

Figure 4.17

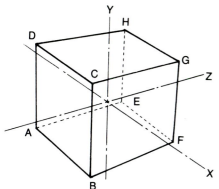

Figure 4.18

	X	Y	Z
A	−200	−200	−200
B	200	−200	−200
C	200	200	−200
D	−200	200	−200
E	−200	−200	200
F	200	−200	200
G	200	200	200
H	−200	200	200

Program 4.14

```
 10 MODE0
 20 VDU23;8202;0;0;0;
 30 VDU29,640;512;
 40 VP=-700::scale=150
 50 FOR ANGLE=10 TO 60 STEP5
 60 CLS
 70 Sin=SINRAD(-ANGLE)
 80 Cos=COSRAD(-ANGLE)
 90 READ N
100 FOR I=1 TO N
110 READ X,Y,Z,plot
120 X=X*scale:Y=Y*scale:Z=Z*scale
130 PROCplot(plot,X,Y,Z)
140 NEXT
150 KEY=GET
160 RESTORE:NEXT ANGLE
170 END
180 DATA 16
190 DATA 1,-1,-1,4
200 DATA 1,1,-1,5
210 DATA -1,1,-1,5
220 DATA -1,-1,-1,5
230 DATA 1,-1,-1,5
240 DATA 1,-1,1,5
250 DATA 1,1,1,5
260 DATA 1,1,-1,5
270 DATA 1,1,1,4
280 DATA -1,1,1,5
290 DATA -1,1,-1,5
300 DATA -1,-1,-1,4
310 DATA -1,-1,1,5
320 DATA -1,1,1,5
330 DATA -1,-1,1,4
340 DATA 1,-1,1,5
350 DEF PROCplot(plot,X,Y,Z)
360 x=X*Cos-Z*Sin:z=Z*Cos+X*Sin
370 y=Y*Cos-z*Sin:z=z*Cos+Y*Sin
380 F=VP/(VP-z)
390 PLOTplot,x*F,y*F
400 ENDPROC
```

The following is a brief explanation of the lines of the program:

- 10   Sets MODE 0.
- 20   Switches off flashing cursor.
- 30   Sets the graphics origin at the centre of the screen.
- 40   Sets the variables. VP is the distance of the viewing point from the origin and 'scale' is a scaling factor for the lengths of the sides.

50	Sets up a loop which will allow the cube to be rotated at angles from 0 to 60 degrees in steps of 5.
60	Clears the screen.
70–80	Converts the angles into radians.
90	READs the number of lines (N) from the first DATA statement in line 180.
100	Sets up a loop to get values for X, Y, Z and 'plot' from DATA lines 190–340.
110	READs the values.
120	Places X,Y and Z values as unit values in the DATA lines and scales them up by multiplying by the value 'scale' which is set in line 40.
130	Calls PROCEDURE to draw the cube.
140	Goes back to line 100 to get new data and draw the next line.
150	Waits for a key to be pressed.
160	Ensures that the data is read from the beginning again.
170	Marks the end of the program.
180–340	DATA lines. The first three numbers in each line give unit values for the sides and the fourth number gives the PLOT number to be used in line 380.
350	Defines the PROCEDURE 'plot' to draw the cube.
360–370	Calculates the x,y and z co-ordinates from the X, Y and Z values.
380	Calculates the perspective scaling factor, F. For realistic 3D projection the lines of the cube are made to converge as they get further away from the eye. This perspective scaling depends on the distance of the observer from the centre of the object. The scaling is produced here by multiplying each x and y co-ordinate by a perspective scaling factor, F.
390	Draws lines or moves to the calculated x and y co-ordinates depending on the plot value read from the DATA lines. PLOT 4 moves without drawing a line and PLOT 5 draws a line.
400	End of PROCEDURE.

Figure 4.19 shows the image obtained from program 4.14.

This type of three dimensional wire-frame drawing can be very confusing; it is greatly clarified if the hidden lines are removed. Programming the computer to work out which lines are not visible at any time can be quite complex. An easy way to overcome the problem, in this case, is to draw the cube without the lines that would not be visible. This can be achieved by changing line 180 to

180 DATA 11

This will alter the program so that the computer only draws the visible lines, as illustrated in Figure 4.20.

This is a very simple example of three-dimensional graphics but it demonstrates some of the principles involved. It should also give an idea of the difficulties that occur in producing good-quality three-dimensional graphics when many complex mathematical formulae and vast amounts of data need to be held and manipulated by the computer.

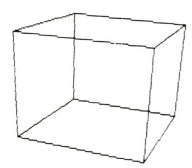

Figure 4.19

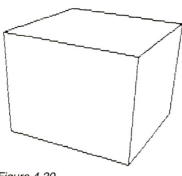

Figure 4.20

5 Commercial systems for schools

The programs presented in this book are deliberately kept quite short so that their structure and operation may be understood and so that they can easily be entered into the computer. Much more sophisticated graphics can be obtained on the BBC micro using commercial computer graphics packages. Although some of these are frequently referred to as CAD packages many are, in fact, computer drafting packages. True CAD facilities would allow the user to design three-dimensionally, view and easily modify objects. Most of the programs available for the BBC, however, only offer facilities for computer-aided drafting.

In this chapter we will look at some of the better-known commercial packages. Each one will be briefly described, and examples of outputs from the packages will be shown. These packages are quite sophisticated and offer more facilities than can be illustrated in the space available here.

There are many more systems available and their exclusion here in no way implies that they have nothing to offer. The packages included are found in many schools and they will serve to make those not familiar with the **software** aware of their existence and the opportunity so see examples of the graphics that can be produced with them.

5.1 The AMX mouse

This was probably one of the first and is one of the best known of the mouse packages for the BBC microcomputer. Advanced Memory Systems have produced some excellent software to accompany the

The AMX mouse

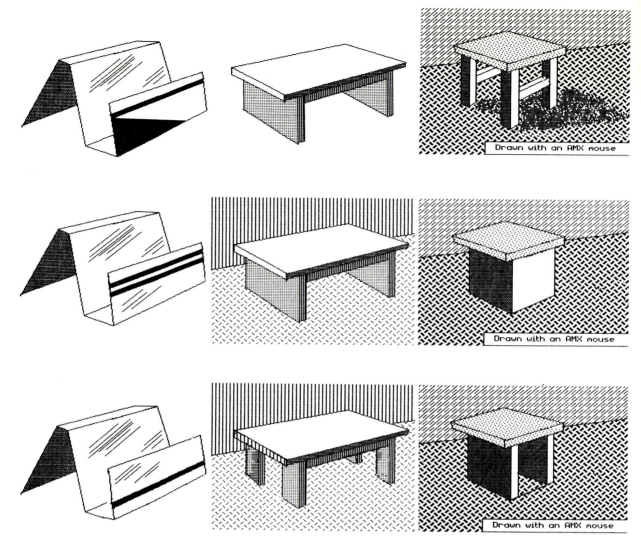

Figure 5.1 Drawings produced with the AMX mouse using the Super Art Software

mouse. The packages which would be most directly related to CDT are AMX Super Art, 3D Zicon and AMX Design.

AMX Super Art allows a variety of drawings to be constructed with rectangle- and circle-drawing facilities provided (see Figure 5.1). Lettering can be added in a variety of styles, and there is an interesting selection of texture patterns which can be used to infill areas. There is also a facility for defining and storing **icons** which can be used for a variety of drawing purposes including the production of circuit diagrams. This is a reasonably priced, fun package, which can be used to produce a variety of interesting graphics.

The 3D Zicon package allows three-dimensional images to be created and rotated. The package is relatively inexpensive and as such has obvious limitations in the quality of images it can produce and it is restricted by the limitations imposed by the BBC microcomputer.

AMX Design is a two-dimensional drafting package which will allow the drawing of printed circuit boards (PCBs) and intricate orthographic projections. Full zoom and macro facilities are included, and drawings can be output to a range of printers and plotters.

5.2 British Thornton Compas

This is really a system of packages which allows the user to begin with a relatively simple CAD package, Compas Starter, and progress to the ultimate Compas Advanced, which offers many of the facilities used in professional systems. The advanced system is complex and has a substantial manual. Full understanding of the facilities and their operation takes some time, but this is to be expected with a system that offers so many facilities. Compas Advanced offers facilities for two-dimensional drafting with three-dimensional viewing and an option to attach and drive a **Computer Numerically Controlled (CNC)** lathe. The input can be via a mouse or **digitising tablet**, and the system offers all the facilities associated with this level of computer-aided drafting, including lines and curves, automatic dimensioning, shape dragging and display of co-ordinates. In addition to these facilities three-dimensional views of pre-defined two-dimensional objects can be developed quickly and then viewed in a variety of three-dimensional projections. Views from any position around the object or even from within it can be obtained by selecting the point of view and centre of interest.

British Thornton CAM

This is a CAD/CAM package which allows the user to draw accurate profiles and then view them as three-dimensional wireframes. The program will also generate the machine 'G-Code' program which can be utilised on a variety of training lathes including Boxford and Denford. A screen simulation of the machining sequence is included so that the user can experience computer drafting integrated with automatic generation of G-Code programs and machining sequence simulation without having a CNC machine connected.

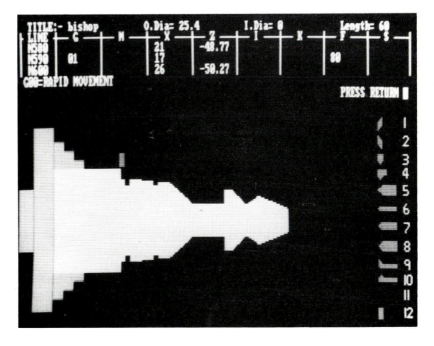

Boxford CAM machining simulation

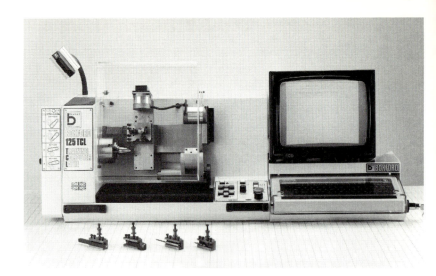

The Boxford 125 TCL which can be used with British Thornton's CAM

5.3 Easidraw, Easicad and Easicam

Easidraw is a low-cost beginner's drawing package which is **menu-driven** by a **tracker ball**. Circles, boxes, triangles and lines can be drawn to co-ordinate positions for building shapes accurately. The freehand mode allows sketching, and a colour-fill routine enhances drawings produced. The drawings can be saved for future use and/or printed out on most dot matrix printers. Text may be added in lower or upper case and in a condensed upper case in any of the colours available. Errors can be deleted with an area erasing facility.

Easicad is a powerful CAD/CAM system which has been designed by Metrosoft Ltd for the BBC range of microcomputers. It is a sophisticated, easy-to-use, two-dimensional computer-aided drafting package. The user can create drawings interactively by selecting drawing features from a menu and locating lines, arcs and so on on the screen

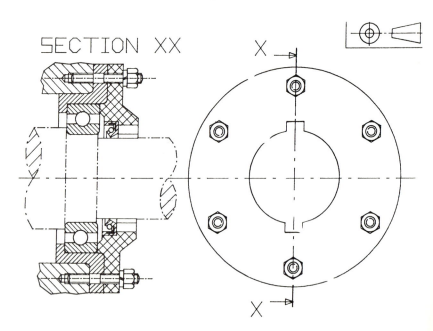

Figure 5.2 A plotter dump from Easicad

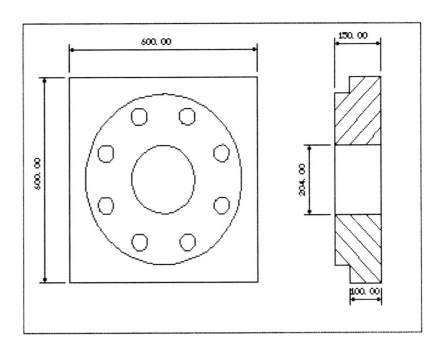

Figure 5.3 Screen dumps to a dot matrix printer from Easicad

by moving a cross-wire cursor using either the Marconi Tracker Ball or **keyboard co-ordinate input** and/or a **digitiser stylus**. Drawings from A4 to A0 may be prepared at scales from 100:1 to 1:100. When the drawing is complete it may be plotted on most plotters or screen-dumped to a dot matrix printer for quick reference.

Easidraw and Easicad are produced by Metrotec Ltd, Sunderland.

Easicam is a comprehensive software link between CAD and CNC milling and turning. The user can take the Easicad shape and interactively define the machining process, check the machining graphically, then produce the part on a CNC machine.

5.4 Grafpad 2

The software is not unlike that of the AMX mouse, offering many similar facilities with a selection of textured shading patterns for infilling. The main difference is the input device, which is a digitising tablet as shown on page 65. This consists of a flat board with a grid marked on it and a stylus which is used to draw and select options. The movement of the stylus on the board is traced out on the VDU.

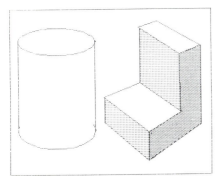

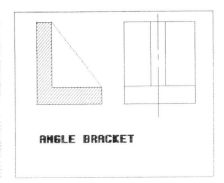

Figure 5.4 Examples produced with the Grafpad 2

Figure 5.5 A screen shot from Vehicle Design

5.5 Vehicle Design (Heinemann)

This is a program which allows the user to check the aerodynamic effectiveness of car body shapes. The program offers pre-drawn shapes which can be selected for testing or the user can design and draw original forms. The shape can be given a simulated wind tunnel test to obtain a drag coefficient and then the design can be modified if necessary. This program is ideal for use with projects in years 1 to 3 where vehicle body design is involved.

5.6 Designer (Techsoft, Clwyd)

This is a powerful and versatile computer-aided drafting package which comes on two ROMs. The program offers all the facilities expected from the more sophisticated CAD packages for the BBC microcomputer including a variety of line and arc drawing commands, powerful delete facilities, zoom, automatic dimensioning, move and rotate commands.

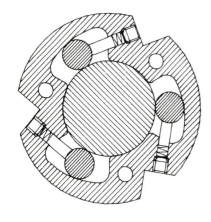

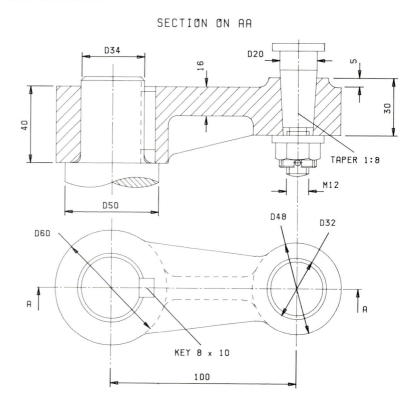

Figure 5.6 Drawings produced by TECHSOFT DESIGNER

5.7 Linear Graphics

Linear Graphics make the Plotmate plotter and have produced a variety of accompanying software.

Lincad

This is a drafting package which offers many of the facilities already mentioned in some of the previous drafting systems.

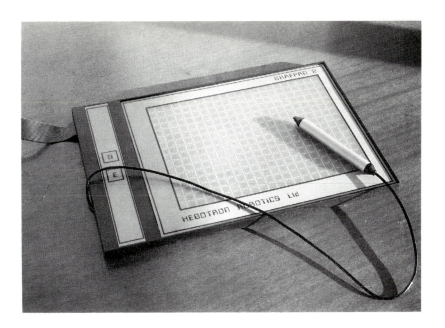

The Grafpad 2 digitising tablet

Lintronics

This software allows the user to draw, save and label electronic circuits using the extensive selection of electronic symbols provided, and to draw them out on a Plotmate plotter. The diagrams which have been saved on disk may be recalled at any time for modification and reprinting.

Lintrack

This extremely useful package lets the user design and draw out **PCB** artwork. A variety of track widths and pad sizes can be selected, and once the PCB layout has been designed on the screen the artwork can be produced on tracing film using a Plotmate plotter with a Rotring or similar drawing pen fitted. Special pen adaptors are available for this purpose.

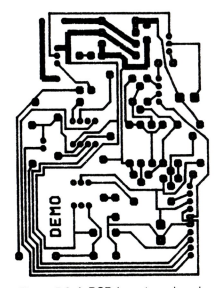

Figure 5.8 A PCB layout produced on a Plotmate plotter using the Lintrack software

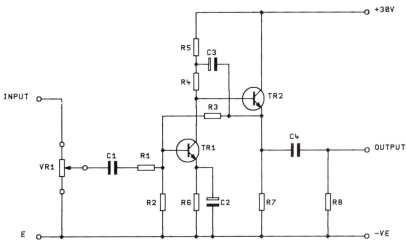

Figure 5.7 Line Amp Circuit by Plotmate produced with Lintronics on a Plotmate plotter

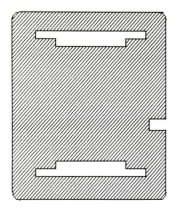

5.8 MICAD (Heinemann)

This is an inexpensive software package which has provided many schools with their first experience of computer-aided drafting. The package consists of two programs called MICAD 2D and MICAD 3D.

MICAD 2D is a two-dimensional drafting program which offers facilities for producing lines, arcs and circles, hatching, zooming, grids, scaling and auto-dimensioning. Text may be added at any angle and size, and the drawings can be edited, stored, retrieved and printed or plotted out.

MICAD 3D allows wire-frame representations of simple solid shapes to be constructed and viewed from a variety of angles. The drawings are very elementary and there is no hidden line removal, which can lead to confusing images.

5.9 Pineapple Software

Diagram

Diagram is a useful program which allows large amounts of information both in diagrammatic and text form to be stored on a **floppy disk**. This program is particularly suitable for applications which require both graphics and text to be mixed and also require more drawing space than can be fitted into a single MODE 0 screen of the BBC micro. Up to 128 shapes and symbols can be pre-defined for any diagram, and any one can be selected from a screen display to be printed at the cursor position. The program is compatible with the Marconi tracker ball, and with the use of a special adaptor lead the AMX mouse can also be used.

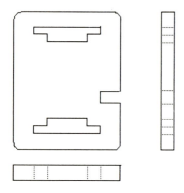

Figure 5.9 Drawings produced by MICAD

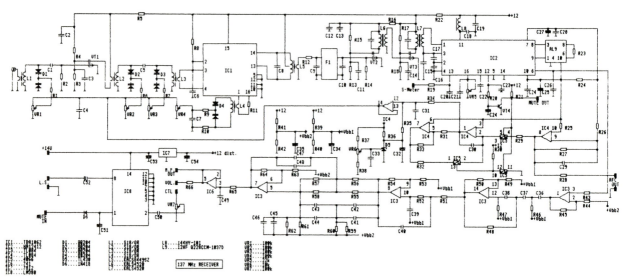

Figure 5.10 An example produced with Diagram from Pineapple Software

PCB

PCB is a program which will allow high-quality artwork for the production of both single-sided and double-sided PCBs. The program comes on a ROM, which has to be plugged into one of the ROM sockets in the computer. Individual **pads** and **IC pads** can be selected from a menu and moved about the screen for location on the board. An automatic routing facility is available on a second ROM. Labelling can be added to boards, and there are comprehensive erasing techniques for correcting mistakes.

The program prints out on Epson-compatible dot matrix printers, and the print routine produces a very accurate and dense image which can be used as the original mask if the paper is sprayed with WD40 to make it transparent or if a photocopy is made on to transparent film. Printing directly on to suitable tracing paper also produces a PCB mask.

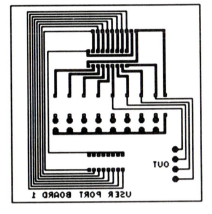

Figure 5.11 PCB artwork produced with Pineapple Software's PCB

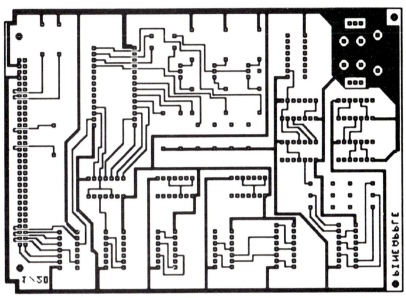

5.10 Robocom Bitstik

This is a powerful and versatile drafting package which offers many facilities to simplify the task of producing, storing and modifying draw-

The Bitstik controller

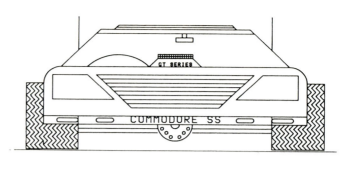

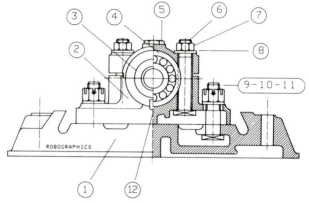

Figure 5.12 Examples of drawings produced with the Robocom Bitstik

ings. The system is based around a control 'stick' which is similar to a joystick but is custom-designed for this system.

As with most sophisticated packages, the Bitstik system takes some time before it can be used to advantage. It is 'menu driven', which means that most of the options can be selected from a menu or list which appears on the screen. As well as offering a variety of line and curve-drawing facilities to simplify the task of creating drawings, the system also offers automatic dimensioning, zooming and a sophisticated library. This allows the user to store any drawing, which can then be copied into any other drawing at any chosen position and to any scale. These drawings can also be rotated, with stretching or mirroring should they be required. This library system has many applications and can speed up the production of drawings and circuit diagrams.

The software also enables drawings to be produced on all of the more popular plotters, which results in a high-quality image. There is also the option to produce 'hard copies' on a dot matrix printer if a plotter is not available, but the quality of the output is not very satisfactory and it is not appropriate for such a sophisticated system

Further reading

Books

The following books give many more details about **computer graphics**:

N. P. and A. Cryer, *Graphics on the BBC Microcomputer*, Prentice/Hall International, 1983.

J. McGregor and Alan Watt, *The Art of Microcomputer Graphics*, Addison-Wesley, 1985.

A. Oldknow, *Graphics and Microcomputers*, Nelson, 1985.

The following will help with **general programming**:

John Coll, *The BBC Microcomputer User Guide*, The British Broadcasting Corporation, 1982.

David Smith, *BBC Basic for Beginners*, Melbourne House Publishers, 1983.

Journals

There are many journals for computer users available and several are devoted to the BBC microcomputer. Useful articles about graphics appear in all of them from time to time, but the author has found the *Acorn User* particularly helpful as it has regularly featured articles concerning computer graphics.

Glossary

ASCII This is short for American Standard Code for Information Interchange. This is a system which gives each key on the computer keyboard a code number. The word 'ASCII' (pronounced 'askey') is formed from the first letter from each of the words in the full name. This type of word is called an acronym.

Axes The plural of axis which is a line used as a reference point. In geometry two axes at right angles are used to locate points in a plane. The vertical axis is known as the Y axis and the horizontal one the X axis.

BASIC Another acronym (see ASCII), this time formed from Beginners All-purpose Symbolic Instruction Code which is a type of computer language developed for beginners to learn how to program computers.

CNC This is the term used to describe computer-controlled machines and it stands for Computer Numerically Controlled.

Cursor A small movable symbol on a visual display unit which locates a position.

Digital data Information which is stored as a series of electrical impulses. 1 indicates a voltage, 0 indicates no voltage. Computers store all their data and perform all their calculations digitally using a series of 1s and 0s.

Digitiser stylus An electronic pen which is used to input data into a computer. This is usually used with a special **digitising tablet** (see below) to produce graphics on a computer.

Digitising tablet Used with a stylus to input data into a computer. It is a plastic pad which is usually marked with a grid and various control areas. There is a wire grid inside designed to allow the computer to locate the position of a special **digitising stylus** which is used to 'draw' on the tablet. This piece of equipment is often used to help the user to draw with a computer.

Disk interface A number of ICs (Integrated Circuits) which have to be in the computer before a disk drive can be connected so that programs and information can be saved and loaded into the computer from a disk.

Dot matrix printer The most common type of printer used with computers. The alphabet is formed by a rectangular set or matrix of wire needles which are pushed out in differing sequences to form shapes for all the letters, numerals and other symbols a computer can form.

Floppy disk This is a disk of thin magnetic material which is similar to the tape used in audio cassettes. The disk is usually 5.25 inches in diameter and is held in a protective card sleeve. The surface of the disk is sensitive and should be treated with care to make sure that information stored on it is not destroyed.

Graphics co-ordinate system A system used to locate points in a plane using two **axes** (see above) which are at right-angles to each other. One is vertical and is called the Y axis and the other is horizontal and is called the X axis. Points are located within the axes just like positions are given on a map using horizontal and vertical co-ordinates.

Graphics cursor This is a movable point which indicates a position on the screen. The BBC computer has an invisible graphics cursor which moves around the screen in very small steps. Programs can be written to place a visible cursor on the screen which, for graphics, is usually a small cross.

Graphics dump ROM This is an Integrated Circuit which contains a program to get anything appearing on the **visual display unit** printed out on a printer.

Graphics tablet This is another term for a **digitising tablet**.

Hardware The actual pieces of equipment used for computing, for example the computer, printer, plotter and disk drive.

Hexadecimal A system of counting using 16 as a base instead of our usual 10. Computer programming is often made simpler by using hexadecimal numbers. These numbers usually have the & symbol placed in front of them to show that they are using a base of 16. Therefore, & 52 would represent $5 \times 16 + 2$ in our usual base 10 counting. That is & $52 = 82_{10}$.

IC pads IC is short for Integrated Circuit or Chip. These are now at the heart of most electronic devices and when planning **printed circuit boards**, which connect the various components together, small disks are used to locate the position of components. The two parallel rows of legs on the ICs have to be carefully soldered into the **printed circuit boards** and their location is fixed at the planning stage with the use of the small disks which are called pads.

Icons These are small computer images which are used as symbols to represent things.

Interactive drafting Drawing systems in which the computer offers alternatives from which the user can make selections. Using these systems the computer and the user interact to provide a more flexible system.

Joystick A 'stick' which controls the movement of figures around the screen. Most commonly used for computer games but it can be useful for computer graphics.

Keyboard co-ordinate input This term is used when graphics co-ordinates, which give the position of images on the **visual display unit**, are located by pressing keys on the computer keyboard.

Light pen A device which looks like a pen, but contains a light sensitive circuit. When used with suitable **software** it can be used to produce graphics on the **visual display unit**.

Menu-driven A menu shows the user all the options that are available from a program and allows easy selection of any of those options. Menu-driven means the program can be controlled from a menu which is always visible or is easily brought on to the **visual display unit**.

Mouse A small input device which usually has three buttons and because of this and its shape, along with the connecting lead going to the computer, looks similar to a mouse. It has a small ball on its underside which is rolled around on a surface and this movement can be detected by the computer. The mouse is used as an alternative to a **joystick** or **graphics tablet** for controlling movement on the **visual display unit**.

Pads These are used in laying out **printed circuit boards**. They are small disks with holes in the centre which locate the position of components on the boards.

PCB Short for printed circuit boards. This is the way that all commercial electronic components are put together to form working circuits. The components are linked with copper tracks or connecting lines and the components themselves are soldered into **pads** on the board.

Pixel A small, illuminated, rectangular area on a **visual display unit**.

Plotout A computer generated drawing which is drawn out by a **plotter**.

Plotter This is a device which the computer can control to reproduce screen drawings accurately using drawing pens.

Rectangular Cartesian set Another name for the **Graphics co-ordinate system** which was developed by Descartes, the seventeenth-century French mathematician.

ROM Short for **Read Only Memory**. This is an Integrated Circuit programmed so that the instructions it contains can be read by the computer but it cannot easily be erased.

Screen dump ROM A ROM containing information which will allow the computer to get anything appearing on the **visual display unit** printed out by a printer.

Screen prompt A message which appears on the screen to help or tell the user what to do.

Software Programs which allow the computer to perform various tasks.

Systems disk A **floppy disk** containing **software** produced by manufacturers to drive their **hardware**.

Text cursor The small flashing rectangle on the **visual display unit** which indicates where text will be printed.

Tracker ball Another type of input device which is particularly useful for graphics. It is rather like an upside down **mouse** where the moving ball is on the top and is rotated by the user to move lines and shapes around the screen.

Visual display unit Often called a VDU for short. This is the way we can see what the computer is doing and it is basically a television screen. Many people use their ordinary televisions as VDUs but special screens are produced for computers to give clearer images.

Wire frame The simplest form of three-dimensional image produced by computers. The picture is made up of a series of lines which make the solid image look like it has been modelled in wire.